Paul and Denise Burton

walk & eat
LISBON

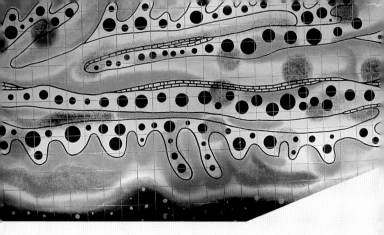

This pocket guide is designed for short-break walking holidays from Lisbon, using the excellent public transport network (or a car, if you prefer). Fly out for just a week or a long weekend. You have in your hand enough walks, excursions, restaurants and recipes to last two weeks — so you can pick and choose the most appealing.

The highlights at a glance:

- 10 varied day walks, each with topographical map
- 2 excursions — one to the Tagus Estuary Natural Park, the other to the medieval walled town of Óbidos
- recommended restaurants for the walks and excursions
- recipes to make at your self-catering base or back home
- special section with hints on wheat-, gluten- and dairy-free eating and cooking in the Lisbon area

There is little doubt that Lisbon has risen significantly in the European capital popularity stakes in recent years, and deservedly so! Hosting Expo98 and the 2004 European Football Championship helped enormously, not only in promoting the city as an attractive destination, but also as catalysts in improving tourist infrastructures. Travelling within the city and to the surrounding areas, whether by public or private transport, has been made immeasurably more visitor-friendly as a direct result of hosting these major events.

Building on this, our book does not attempt to be a general guide to the city itself — there are many of these — instead, we provide practical information on using Lisbon as a base for walking and eating in the wider 'Costa de Lisboa' (Lisbon Coast) region.

Extending from Peniche in the north to Sesimbra and Setúbal in the south and to the River Tagus in the east, the **Costa de Lisboa**, linked geographically and commercially to Lisbon, offers a wonderful variety of scenery, culture and an insight into the rich heritage of Portuguese history.

The pre-historical presence of dinosaurs near Lourinhã, the early Phoenician use of Lisbon as a port of call on their trading routes north, the Roman occupation of Lisbon, followed by the Moors, their conquest in 1147 and finally the establishment of Lisbon as capital of Portugal in 1255, are all events that have left their mark — from fossils to archaeological remains to the imposing Castelo São Jorge in Lisbon and Moors' Castle in Sintra.

But it doesn't end there; with the establishment of Portugal as a nation, this landscape became indelibly marked by the hand of man through the colourful events of national history. Magnificent palaces like Mafra (Walk 9), medieval towns like Óbidos (Excursion 2), the Peninsula Wars (also Walk 9), and the establishment of Sintra (Walk 2) as a place of retreat from Lisbon — all these and many more have influenced the landscape, architecture and way of life we see today.

THE WALKS

There are walks in this book for everyone; from easy, generally flat routes to moderate upland hikes. They have been chosen because they can be *easily reached by public transport from Lisbon and because they offer good eating en route.* In addition, the walks attempt to offer variety of scenery and interest; some following a specific theme — such as dinosaurs at Lourinhã or the Peninsula Wars at Mafra.

THE EXCURSIONS

We have suggested two 'day out' excursions from Lisbon. One takes you by ferry across the Tagus Estuary to Montijo, where you join the bus service to Alcochete, the gateway to the Tagus Estuary Natural Park. Enjoy seeing flamingos and other birdlife from the Interpretation Centre, returning to Lisbon after lunch.

The second is a bus ride north to the beautiful medieval town of Óbidos. When you see it you will understand why for centuries Portuguese kings offered the town as a wedding gift to their brides. Not only does Óbidos preserve its architectural integrity almost perfectly, but it also offers plenty of good restaurants.

Authors' Note

Our first association with Portugal was in 1969, but we have been permanent residents since 1980. There have been enormous changes in the country over this period and, in many ways, Lisbon and the Tagus Valley have perhaps witnessed the greatest transformation — with the area now being at or even above the European average on a whole series of economic indicators.

This progress has had a significant impact on the adjacent landscape, with a rush to build new property across huge swathes of countryside. People here now have cars, time and money for recreation; this becomes very apparent at weekends, with the coast and the Serra de Sintra becoming almost overwhelmed with day-trippers — in stark contrast to much of the rest of Portugal. However, this pressure on the countryside does have its benefits, not least because paths are being waymarked and, through regular use, kept open and maintained.

Back in 1991 Brian and Eileen Anderson wrote a pioneering walking guide in the 'Landscapes' series to the area around Lisbon. When it became out-of-date, the Andersons were were unable to take on the task of revision. Sunflower then approached us, following publication of our *Landscapes of Northern Portugal,* to cover much the same area for the 'walk & eat' series.

We would like to thank the Andersons for allowing us to draw on their excellently-researched text concerning the walks around Sintra, and for their ongoing help with plant identification.

Apart from the Andersons, we would like to thank the staff and officials at the Parque Natural da Arrábida and the Reserva Natural do Estuário do Tejo for all their help, and the Instituto Geográfico do Exército, for their permission to adapt their maps for the walking routes.

THE RESTAURANTS

Based on personal experience, we have recommended at least one restaurant for each walk and excursion. As well as a description of the restaurant, we give a typical summary menu, highlighting their specialities where appropriate. A price guide is given (€ to €€€), to indicate 'very reasonable' to 'fairly pricey'. But remember that you can have a relatively inexpensive meal in quite 'up market' establishments by selecting the *prato do dia*

Rainbows of fish — the mainstay of the Portuguese diet

(dish of the day) or the *ementa turistica* (tourist menu), topped off with *vinho de casa* (house wine). Frequently a light lunch taken in this way can cost less than €12 per person.

Eating out in the evenings is generally more expensive, as there is usually no *prato do dia* available. It is also worth remembering that many restaurants will serve you half-portions *(meia dose)* if you ask; indeed, in Portugal full portions can often be daunting and will put paid to post-lunch walking!

Remember that by law all restaurants are supposed to remain closed for at least one day of the week. We have indicated wherever possible which day this was at the time of writing. *No restaurant has paid — in cash or kind — to be included in this guide.* Our choice is based strictly on personal taste and experience; inclusion (or exclusion) should be so interpreted.

THE RECIPES

The recipes selected from the menus of the various restaurants we feature have been chosen to offer as wide a spectrum of dishes as possible. Being near the coast, almost all restaurants feature fresh fish prominently. But in order to achieve an *overall balance* in the recipes, we will describe one of the restaurant's meat dishes, even though they clearly specialise in fish. Rest assured that they *do* also serve meat.

Restaurant staff, and chefs in particular, are nearly always ready and happy to talk about their food and its preparation. There is, however, an understandable reluctance to divulge every last secret of how a dish is prepared. We have gathered as much information as possible and then built on this by cooking the dishes — often more than once — at home, to ensure that they are workable. This has proved to be a considerable challenge for Denise who, being a vegetarian, has suddenly had to face preparing a whole host of meat dishes which she would not normally have contemplated!

Sunflower's request for special consideration to be given to readers with food intolerances was another hurdle, but we

> ### Recommended cookery books
>
> *Portuguese Home Cooking* by Maria Carma Brás Lournço Alves (ISBN 972-99198-1) covers 8 regions of Portugal, describing a total of 16 regional dishes.
>
> *A Taste of Portugal* by Nica Paixão (ISBN 972-8748-10-8) is a voyage into Portuguese culture and tradition.
>
> *Portuguese Cooking* (ISBN 88-476-0921-6) is a well-illustrated introduction to regional dishes, with a background history of Portugal.

hope our recipes — all of which can be made **gluten- and dairy-free** (see page 139) will be of real help and enable them to enjoy to the full their excursions and walks with us.

PORTUGUESE FOOD

Portuguese food is a wonderful mix of the Mediterranean and Atlantic, both in terms of the contrasting fish and shellfish and the produce from the land itself, which 'hovers' between these two ecosystems. Moreover there is often the hint of Africa, Brazil or the Orient in the cooking, due partly to historical links but also, and especially around Lisbon, the more recent influx of migrant workers.

Apart from *bacalhau* (dried cod; see page 136) and **smoked meat** (sausages, hams, etc), nearly all Portuguese cooking relies heavily on **good fresh produce**. The market gardens to the north (seen, for example, on Walk 10) are testimony to this, as are the well-stocked markets of Lisbon. Fresh **fish** and **shellfish** are also available in incredible variety and abundance.

Cured hams and smoked pigs' trotters in a Lisbon market

With the passage of time it becomes more difficult to identify which dishes truly originated in Lisbon as opposed to other parts of the country. Certainly *bacalhau à Brás* (see page 32) is a Lisbon creation, as is *amêijoas à Bulhão Pato* (see page 105). But many dishes served in and around Lisbon are available throughout Portugal, and their true geographic origin is lost in history.

PORTUGUESE WINES

To complement a meal, whether in a restaurant or in self-catering, Portuguese wines offer an amazing choice. Many of the better wines are still relatively unknown outside Portugal, so a restaurant wine list or supermarket shelf may look quite bewildering, with few recognisable names.

The Costa de Lisboa to the north and west of the Tagus produces the **Estremadura Regional Wines** ('Vinho Regional' on the label). Within this region there are specific Demarcated (sub)Regions ('VPQRD' on the label), such as Lourinhã, Óbidos, Alenquer, Torres Vedras, Bucelas and Colares. As a general

Try these!

Wines from Estremadura

- Quinta de Abrigada Tinto (DOC)
- Valle do Riacho Tinto or Branco (VQPRD)
- Tinta Roriz Tinto
- Aba da Serra Tinto

Colares
Casal de Azenha tinto — particularly good value

Bucelas
Quinta do Avelar

Glossary

DOC: wine from a demarcated region;
VPQRD: quality wine from a demarcated sub-region;
Regional: wine from a DOC area, but not using recognised grapes;
garrafa: bottle;
rolha: cork (in case you want to take it home!)

Tip: A highly readable account of Portuguese wine (with an excellent historical section that encompasses much more than just viniculture), *The Wines and Vineyards of Portugal* by Richard Mayson (Mitchell Beazley, 2003) is not to be missed.

11

rule, the VPQRD wines tend to be made predominantly with *national* grape varieties, while the Regional wines frequently contain some of the better-known *international* grape varieties blended in.

Apart from the better-known white *(branco)* wines from Bucelas (25km north of Lisbon) and the small remaining production of red *(tinto)* from Colares, the Estremaduran wines have begun to receive attention only relatively recently. Many producers have significantly improved quality, and there are some excellent wines now available from this little-known region.

To the south of the Tagus lies the 'Terras do Sado' wine region, within which is the Setúbal sub-region (with the longest history of wine production in Iberia), famous for its Moscatel de Setúbal, a sweet fortified wine.

Wines to look out for from further afield include the (generally) *lighter reds* from the Douro (Esteva, Evel, Tuella, Dorna Velha, Duas Quintas) or the much *heavier reds* from the Alentejo (Borba, Esporão, Mouchão). For *whites* try Planalto (Douro), João Pires (Palmela/Alentejo) or, from the far north, an Alvarinho *vinho verde.*

PLANNING YOUR VISIT
When to go

Lisbon is worth visiting at any time of the year, but winter (especially November to March) can be foggy, misty and rainy. This is not a great problem for visiting the city itself (or enjoying some of our restaurants), but is likely to make walking in the surrounding countryside less enjoyable. Even so, there can be fine, sunny spells throughout the winter, although these are difficult to predict.

Most Lisboetas go on holiday in August, and while there is far less traffic congestion in the city itself, nearby coastal resorts such as Cascais and Estoril can be very crowded.

For walking probably the best time of year is **spring/early summer** (April to June). The weather is generally good, and the temperatures not too high. Above all, the countryside is most vividly coloured at this time.

Autumn, too, is good for walking, but days become shorter and, beyond mid-October, the weather can be unpredictable.

Averages	Jan	Feb	Mar	Apr	May	Jun
Temperature (°C)	11	12	14	15	17	20
Rainfall (mm)	95	87	85	60	46	18
Averages	**Jul**	**Aug**	**Sep**	**Oct**	**Nov**	**Dec**
Temperature (°C)	22	23	22	19	15	12
Rainfall (mm)	4	5	33	75	100	97

Where to stay

Lisbon has a huge selection of accommodation from luxury hotels to humble *residências*. For easy access via public transport to the walks described in this book, choose accommodation near the **city centre**. An alternative, if you only intend doing the walks to the north of Lisbon, might be to stay at **Sintra**, which has good public transport links to most of the walks. If you have your own transport, you could well consider staying in one of the excellent *Turismo Rural* properties outside Lisbon.

Alternatively you might like to try self-catering accommodation. There's plenty available; just search 'Lisbon apartment
rental' on the internet and you will get a wealth of ideas. Then
you'll be able to try some of our recipes using local ingredients!

What to take

Pack simply! Eating out in Portugal, even for dinner, is
generally fairly informal, and the restaurants we list are no
exception — so apart from some smart casuals, concentrate on
packing appropriate walking gear.

While no special equipment is needed for any of the walks,
proper **walking boots** are preferable to any other footwear.
Many walks can become slippery when wet, and some are on
uneven surfaces with loose gravel, so good ankle support is
essential. Paths often have large puddles and can become
streams during or after rain, so good walking boots will help
keep your feet dry. Each person should carry a **small rucksack**,
and *all year round* it is advisable to pack it with a **sunhat, first-
aid kit, spare socks** and some **warm clothing**. A **long-sleeved
shirt** and **long trousers** should be worn or carried, for sun
protection and for pushing your way through encroaching
vegetation (which may be wet and prickly). You should always
carry a **mobile phone**; the **emergency** number in Portugal (as
throughout the EU) is **112**. At least one member of the party
should carry a **compass** (or GPS), and a pair of **compact bino-
culars** can often be helpful in spotting distant waymarks (as
well as birdlife!).

Depending on the season, you may also need a **windproof, lightweight rainwear, fleece** and **gloves**. Optional items include **swimwear** and a **Swiss Army Knife** (packed in your hold luggage, not hand luggage, or it will be confiscated!). Mineral water is sold almost everywhere in plastic half or one-and-a-half litre bottles; *it is imperative that each walker carries at least half a litre of water — a full litre or more in summer*.

If you are self-catering and enjoy your 'cuppa', you may find it worth bringing your own **tea bags**; they are available locally but often of indifferent quality. Don't forget to pack a **UK-to-Continental plug adapter**, and if you are using **film** for photography it is worth bringing a stock with you.

Planning your walks

Look through the walk descriptions in advance; this will help you decide if any additional equipment might be required. The walks are specifically designed for access by the local and regional bus and rail network … so that you can enjoy a bottle of wine with lunch! But if you do want to hire a car, and the route is linear, you can usually leave your car at the end of the walk and then take a bus to the start. Bear in mind that if you are driving and are tempted to imbibe at lunchtime, the **local alcohol limit is 0.5mg/l**, significantly lower than the UK. Police carry out far more random checks than a few years ago and, if you are involved in an accident, you will automatically be breathalysed.

The walks have been **graded** for level of difficulty, but none of them should be beyond the capabilities of anyone who takes moderate and regular exercise. The maximum height gain on any of the walks is 350m, but gradients are generally pretty gentle; any exceptions are specifically mentioned It is important to remember that the times indicated are *neat walking times and do not allow for any stops;* you should probably **allow double the time shown** to take into account photo and refreshment stops.

The **walking maps** are based on the 1:25,000 'Carta Militar' M888 Series published by the Instituto Geográfico do Exército. Most of the sheets are from 1992-1994 and so predate a considerable amount of the road-building and urban development that has taken place in the last ten years, especially immediately north and west of Lisbon. Where necessary we have added detail such as tracks, paths and landmarks to help navigation on the walks.

Walking safely depends in great part on knowing what to expect and being properly equipped. For this reason we urge you to *read through the whole walk description* at your leisure before setting out, so that you have a mental picture of each stage of the route and the landmarks. Some of the walks have been waymarked usually with red/yellow stripes (= means this way, X means not this way, ⌐ means turn right and ⌐ turn left). But beware: waymarking is often poor or confusing, so *always follow our route description.*

Some of the walks do penetrate quite isolated countryside, and none of them is likely to be busy with other walkers (except in the Sintra hills at weekends). It may be quite a while before anyone finds you if you get into difficulty, so our advice is: **never walk alone**.

ON ARRIVAL
Tourist information

Lisbon Airport is very close to the centre of town. There is no metro connection, but plenty of taxis (make sure the meter is set!) and airport buses to the city centre.

There are **tourist information desks** in the arrivals area of the airport, one for Lisbon and another for the whole of Portugal. The main tourist office is in Praça dos Restauradores (1 on the plan inside the front cover), but for really comprehensive information on Lisbon, you should go to the **Lisboa Welcome Centre** in the Praça do Comércio (2 on the plan).

Train times can be obtained from Santa Apolónia station (300m off the east side of the plan) or at www.cp.pt .

All towns have their own tourist information offices from which you will usually be able to get a town plan and tips on any local sites or sights of interest. The major tourist attractions (Sintra, Mafra, Cabo de Roca, etc) also have information offices.

City transport pass

For travel **within Lisbon**, a 'Lisboa Card', valid for 1, 2 or 3 days gives you unlimited travel on the bus and metro services together with entry to many museums and monuments. This is available at airport arrivals, Santa Apolónia station or the Welcome Centre. For full details see www.askmelisboa.com.

For the **Sintra area**, a Scott URB travel pass (€9.00) covers train and bus services in the area; it is available from suburban service railway stations (Cais do Sodre, Alcântara, Belém and

Above and opposite: Mercado da Ribeira

Oriente, in Sintra from the Scotturb ticket office next to Sintra railway station), or from the station ticket office itself. See www.scotturb.com.

Shopping for self-catering

If you are daunted by the Portuguese language, then clearly the answer to shopping, as anywhere, is to head to one of the big 'self-serve' **hypermarkets**. Lisbon has several such shopping centres, and they generally offer excellent quality food in great variety — including fresh fish and shellfish, a great variety of meats, deli counters and bakeries.

These shopping centres also have *natural produce and special diet shops* — for example at the **Centro Comercial Colombo** (Colégio Militar metro station) or **Centro Comercial Vasco da Gama** (Oriente metro station). If you are looking for specialist health foods, however, then head for one of the 13 branches of Celeiro (see page 139).

Markets

For the more adventurous, a visit to the **local market** is *the* way to do your shopping. To help, we have prepared a shopping vocabulary (page 141). One of the best is the **Mercado da Ribeira Nova**, just west of Cais do Sodré station (600 m west of the Praça do Comércio), but you'll find other, smaller food markets dotted around the city.

O DAS REGRAS, POVO DE LISBOA E CORTES DA NAÇÃO

This walk introduces some of Lisbon's essential characteristics and history. It leads from the planned layout of Pombal's Baixa up through older streets to the Castelo São Jorge, dating from the time of the Visigoths and Moors. From this remarkable viewpoint you descend through the confusion of Alfama's steep, narrow alleys to Praça do Comércio, where Lisbon meets the Tagus.

lisbon city

WALK

Start the walk at the **Estação do Rossio** (3 on the plan) closed at the time of writing) and walk through to **Praça Dom Pedro IV**, with the **Teatro Dona Maria II** (4) on your left. Cross the square towards the Rossio metro station opposite and go through the adjacent **Praça da Figueira** just beyond it, from where the statue of **Dom João I** (5) makes an imposing foreground to the Castelo São Jorge crowning the hilltop (photograph opposite).

Leave the Praça da Figueira by following Rua da

Distance: 4.5km/allow up to 4h; see plan inside front cover

Grade: easy-moderate; there are some steep climbs up towards the castle, but you can always 'cheat' if it's too hot by catching the number 28 tram from Praça da Figueira up to Santa Luzia.

Equipment: comfortable walking shoes

Transport: 🚍 or 🚋 to the Estação do Rossio

Refreshments en route: throughout

Opening hours:
Castelo São Jorge (main fortifications) 09.00-18.00 daily
Governor's House (at the castle) 10.00-13.00 and 14.00-18.00 daily

Palma (at the top, north end of the square, beyond the metro station). You pass the Hotel Mundial on your right and soon come into the **Praça Martim Moniz**, a rather soulless and largely modern open space. But head over towards the **Centro Comercial Mouraria** and, just before this, on the left, you will come to the church of **Senhora da Saúde** (6). The fairly simple exterior conceals some beautiful blue and white tiles inside, so it's well worth taking a look.

On leaving the church, walk back down Rua da Senhora da Saúde for about 25 metres and then turn left by the **Salão**

Lisboa (cultural centre) to take the Escadinhas da Saúde ('Little Stairway of Health'). It's a pretty steep climb up — good for your health! — but there are strategically-placed benches if you want to have a breather on the way.

On reaching Rua Marquês de Ponte de Lima turn right and, now on the level, you will come to Largo da Rosa where, on the corner, you will find an old convent and the church of **São Lourenço** (7). Turn left and immediately ahead of you are steps leading up towards the castle (Escadinha do Castelo). But instead of taking these, turn right into Rua das Farinhas, dropping gently into Rua de São Cristovão, where you will come to the church of **São Cristovão** (8). Walk in front of the church and then climb Calçada Conde Marquês Tancos up to the left, past the modern (but abandoned) market of São Loureiro on your right. At the top you will reach the **Bar dos Imagens** (9); pause at this little terrace for your first views out across the city below, framed with vines and attractive verandas off to your left.

Continuing ahead, you will see the Chapitos Acção Social building: pass this and, about 25 metres further on, take the Escadinhas de São Crispim down to the right, passing the **Irish College** (1611; 10 on the plan), which survived the great Lisbon earthquake of 1755. At the bottom, turn right along Rua São Mamede, then take the second left turn, down an unnamed road (it is Travessa Almada). This will bring you steeply down to the church of **Santa Maria Madalena** (11).

From here follow the tramlines uphill along Rua Santo António da Sé, passing the church of Santo António (12) on the left and immediately after, on the next bend, the imposing **Sé** (cathedral; 13 on the plan). Walk to the left of the cathedral, still following the tram lines. You pass the **old prison** (14) on your left and finally come out at the **belvedere** by the church of **Santa Luzia** (15).

Tile mural at the Santa Luzia belvedere and and the charming urinal at Travessa Funil

Notice the fine tile murals both on the church and the belvedere itself, the latter depicting old Lisbon as seen from the river. This is a very pleasant spot to sit for a while and recover from the climb. You can look over the city and to the wide expanse of the Tagus beyond — and down on the mosaics of daily life carrying on in the Alfama district below you.

Opposite Santa Luzia you will see the Travessa da Santa Luzia: follow this up through a small square (Largo do Contador Mor) and continue up Travessa Funil — at the top of which is a charming public urinal. Turn left along Chão da Feira: ahead of you now is the outer entrance to **Castelo de São Jorge** (16 on the plan) and the old residential area surrounding the castle itself. As you pass through, notice the shrine to São Jorge on your left. Just above, on the right, is a Welcome Centre, where you can pick up a

In the grounds of Castelo São Jorge

detailed map of the castle and buy your entrance ticket. A little further up is the Governor's House, which has quite a good selection of books for sale.

You now come to the entrance to the main fortifications, and you can easily spend an hour wandering around in this area, with its wonderful mix of trees, stone columns, statues, old arches and cannons pointing out over the city. The views on all sides are superb. There is an up-market restaurant here, as well as a less expensive cafeteria serving light snacks.

After your visit, retrace your steps to the main entrance; just outside there is a bus stop, should you want to catch transport back down to the city centre.

To continue the walk, turn right along Travessa São Bartolomeu, then left in front of the sports centre. Wind your way back down to Largo do Contador Mor and the church of Santa Luzia. Turn left, following the tram lines to just past the church, where you come to a small **viewpoint and café** (17 on the plan; Largo das Portas da Sol). From here you can take in the views across Alfama, the church of São Vicente (18; burial place for the House of Bragança monarchs) and the church of Santa Engrácia (19) — the National Pantheon which houses, among others, the tombs of Prince Henry the Navigator, Luís Camões and Vasco da Gama.

Return to just by the corner of Santa Luzia Church, then follow the steep stairway (Rua Norberto Araujo) down past a small vine-shrouded fountain to Rua São João da Praça. Turn left here and, after passing through Largo São Rafael, find Rua São Miguel: this brings you shortly to the church of **São Miguel**

Casa dos Bicos: this Renaissance palace (1523) is named for the unusual pointed stones ('bicos') on the façade. The 1755 earthquake destroyed the two top floors, which were not repaired until the 1980s. Exhibitions are sometimes held here.

(20) in a lovely little square dominated by a fine palm tree.

Continue on along Rua São Miguel until you come to another small square with the Rua da Reguiera leading off right. Follow this and, almost immediately, take the narrow flight of steps up to the left (Beco Carneiro). Turning right at the top, you pass a lovely old fountain on your left. Turn up left just after this and you will come up to the church of **Santo Estevão** (21). Turn right here along Rua Santo Estevão, to a small square with a children's playground, where you join Rua Vigário. Turn right down steps which bring you immediately into Rua dos Remédios, where you turn right.

You come down to the **Casa do Fado e Guitarra Portuguesa** and the Largo do Chafariz de Dentro. Carry on along Rua Terreiro do Trigo, passing the **Chafariz d'el Rei** (King's Fountain) and the **Casa dos Bicos** (22), before finally coming into Campo das Cebolas. Carry on into Rua Alfândega, passing the **door of Nossa Senhora da Conceição** (23) — the only part of this church to survive the 1755 earthquake. Continue following

Arcaded ministerial buildings in the Praça do Comércio, dating from the rebuilding of the city after the earthquake by the Marqués de Pombal

the tramlines, to arrive in the magnificent **Praça do Comércio** (2), once the main maritime gate to the city.

Thankfully this is no longer used as a car park: you can walk around the central expanse and really appreciate the beautiful symmetry, with various ministerial buildings occupying three sides and the Tagus the fourth. Walk under the main archway into Rua Augusta; there are plenty of snack bars and restaurants in the streets off either side.

When you reach the junction where Rua Santa Justa crosses pedestrianised Rua Augusta, turn left to come to the **Elevador de Santa Justa** (24). Ride to the top, from where you will get fine views back over to Castelo São Jorge and down to the Praça Dom Pedro IV below. On leaving the lift, just turn up left along Rua do Ouro and back to the **Estação de Rossio**.

Estação Oriente, Parque das Nações

Alternative visits

To see a few of the famous riverside sites and monuments, arm yourself with a large-scale free city plan or a general guidebook and take the metro to **Cais do Sodré** (600 m west of 2 on the plan). Then hop on a tram out to Belém (but beware, this tram route — and the bus equivalent — is notorious for pick-pockets). Then just stroll around the **Jerónimos Monastery**, the modern **Belém Cultural Centre** and the **Torre de Belém**. You may be tempted to walk back along the riverfront, but this is a disappointing option, as you frequently have to divert back to the busy and noisy Avenida da India.

A better idea is to get the tram (or bus) back as far as the **Doca de Santo Amaro** just by the suspension bridge, **Ponte 25 de Abril**. Here you will find a wonderful selection of restaurants, with cuisine from all over the world, in the old warehouses located in front of what is now a yacht marina.

For a complete contrast to the 'historical' monuments, which no visitor to Lisbon should miss, be sure to take in the super-modern **Parque das Nações** (the Expo98 site). It's almost worth going there just for the metro trip — to see the stunning modern *azulejos* (wall tiles) that adorn the stations on the way. On arrival at Oriente, the Parque das Nações metro station, you will come out into the splendid **Oriente** railway station. Walk up onto the

Torre de Belém, with the 25 Abril suspension bridge in the background

mainline platforms to really appreciate the elegant use of steel by the Spanish architect, Santiago Calatrava, who designed it.

Unlike many other Expo sites, Lisbon's has been a great post-Expo success. This more or less derelict area of the city has been transformed into a vibrant community. The shopping centres are always busy, and there are plenty of restaurants and good hotels. And of course, there are the main buildings from Expo still to be seen; not least the **Oceanarium** (the largest in Europe), the **Portugal Pavilion** and the enormous **Pavilião Atlântico** (now used for hosting major indoor events such as masters tennis). The backdrop is the imposing 17km-long **Ponte Vasco da Gama**, built to coincide with Expo98.

Praça Dom Pedro IV and the Café Nicola

There are countless restaurants and snack bars along the route of the walk and alternative visits. For best value, just drop into one of the small restaurants (if it looks busy with locals you can be confident of good food) at about lunch time on any weekday and ask for the *prato do dia* or *diario*. Usually there will be a set lunch-time menu which will include soup, main course and sweet

restaurants

eat

COMIDA DA RIBEIRA
Av 24 de Julho (Mercado)
(210 312 600; fax 210 312 621
www.espacoribeira.pt
Daily except Sundays, lunch and dinner €-€€
Multibanco debit cards only

specialities include *bacalhau cozido com todos* — **salted cod fish** boiled with potatoes, cabbage, onion and egg; or try *bacalhau à Ribeira*, a version of *bacalhau à Brás* (for which we give the recipe on page 32) done their way, with the addition of prawns

another very popular dish is *espeto de lulas e camarão* (a **kebab of squid and prawns**)

if you prefer **meat** there is an *espetada mista* — a kebab of beef, pork and chicken.

for **dessert** *(sobremesa)* there is plenty of choice of fresh fruit — tropical and seasonal — and fruit salad. Or, if you really have a sweet tooth, chocolate mousse or *leite crème* (recipe on page 33), which is very much like *crème brûlée*.

(sometimes also coffee and wine). This all-inclusive meal can cost as little as €4.50 — exceptional value.

Mention has been made on page 19 of the **Mercado da Ribeira Nova** as a good spot to buy fresh ingredients for self-catering. The market has a restaurant on its upper floor.

Comida da Ribeira

Overlooking the busy Ribeira market, this restaurant offers a choice of very fresh fish grilled to order. Since it is at the market itself, vegetables and any other ingredients used in the kitchen are also almost certainly as fresh as they can be. Specialities include dishes using *bacalhau* (salted cod fish), *polvo* (squid) and steaks. On weekday lunchtimes there is a buffet with the choice of a variety of soups, salads, hot dishes and sweets at a very reasonable price. A 'tourist menu' is available, also very reasonably priced. Alternatively you can always choose one of the many traditional dishes on offer. On Thursday, Friday and Saturday you can enjoy your dinner to the sound of live music.

Salt cod Brás-style (bacalhau à Brás)

Soak the cod fish in fresh water for 24 hours, changing the water several times (see the special section on bacalhau on page 136). Skin the fish and take out the bones. Shred the fish into small pieces.

Cut the potatoes into stick-like chips, the onions into fine rings and finely chop the cloves of garlic. Fry the potatoes in hot oil until they brown slightly, then drain on kitchen paper.

In a heavy-based sauce-pan, gently fry the onion and garlic until the onion is soft. Then add the shredded cod fish (with a tablespoon of Madeira).

Add the fried potato chips to the fish mixture, then the seasoned eggs. Stir the mixture with a fork until it becomes creamy and cooked. Put onto a serving dish and sprinkle with chopped parsley. Garnish with black olives and/or the boiled prawns if you wish.

<u>Ingredients (for 4 people)</u>

400 g bacalhau
(salted cod fish)
3 tbsp olive oil
500 g potatoes
6 eggs, lightly beaten
and seasoned with
salt and pepper
3 onions
2 cloves of garlic
tbsp Madeira wine

parsley
cooking oil for frying
the potato chips
black olives
cooked prawns
(optional, for
Ribeira-style, as
shown above)

recipes

eat

Leite-crème (a crème brûlée)

This recipe might prove a little difficult to do in a rented apartment unless you go out and buy a *ferro*, a small iron plate with a handle which can be heated up on the gas. Otherwise, this is one to try at home, when you can get the blowtorch out of the tool shed!

Salt cod Bras-style (opposite) and *leite-crème* (below), as served at Comida da Ribeira

Beat the egg yolks with the caster sugar, flour and a little milk. Sieve the mixture and slowly add the rest of the milk and the lemon peel.

Cook gently on a low heat, stirring all the time. When the mixture begins to boil, turn down the heat and simmer for 2 minutes, stirring continuously. Remove the lemon peel and pour the mixture into a shallow dish or individual dishes and leave to cool.

Before serving sprinkle sugar on the crème and scorch, using by placing a hot *ferro* on top or using a cook's blowtorch — one of those gadgets now fairly widely available and handy for making crème brûlée and browning toppings on other dishes.

Ingredients (for 4 people)
0.5 l milk
100 g caster sugar
4 egg yolks
1 tbsp flour
1 lemon (peel only)
sugar to sprinkle

Our walk takes you from the historic centre of Sintra all the way up to the castle, Pena Palace and on to Cruz Alta. The whole of the walk is within the area designated a UNESCO World Heritage Site in 1995. As you follow in our footsteps, you will appreciate the reasons for this classification.

sintra castles and palaces
WALK

Sintra is little more than half an hour from Lisbon but has a totally different atmosphere. The town itself is made up of three parts: the old historic centre, the 'village' of São Pedro, and the more modern area (Estefânia). Most visitors head straight for the historic centre, by the Palácio Nacional, although Estefânia sees its share of visitors for the fortnightly second-hand market.

The Sintra Hills rise up to their highest point at Cruz Alta (528m) and consist of syenitic and granitic rocks intruded into the lower-lying and surrounding limestone. Being so near the coast, the hills experience the full force of Atlantic wind and rain in winter. This explains the dense vegetation and tree cover (although the exposed western end has little); the climate encouraged past generations to introduce many foreign species of shrubs and trees in the gardens around their country houses.

Distance: 6.3km/3.9mi; 2h06min

Grade: moderate, with a height gain of 350m/1150ft. Generally good under foot on gravel pathways. Plenty of shade along the way. *IGE 1:25,000 M888 Series map, sheet 416*

Equipment: see pages 14-15

Transport: 🚂 from Lisbon to Sintra (very frequent; see page 142), then walk 0.5km to the old centre, or take 🚌 433 or 434. Or 🚗 to Sintra

Refreshments en route:
Sintra and tea house at Pena Palace

Opening times/Prices
Sintra National Palace daily (ex Wed) 10.00-17.30 (last admission 17.00); €4.00

Pena National Palace daily (ex Mon) 10.00-17.30 (last admission 16.30); €6.00 (includes **gardens**)

Queluz National Palace daily (ex Tue) 10.00-17.00 (last admission 16.30); €4.00

Castelo dos Mouros daily 09.30-18.00 (last admission 17.00); €3.50 (includes access to **Monserrate gardens** and **Pena Park**)

Gardens only (Pena Palace and Moors' Castle) daily 09.30-18.00 (last admissions 17.00); €3.50 each

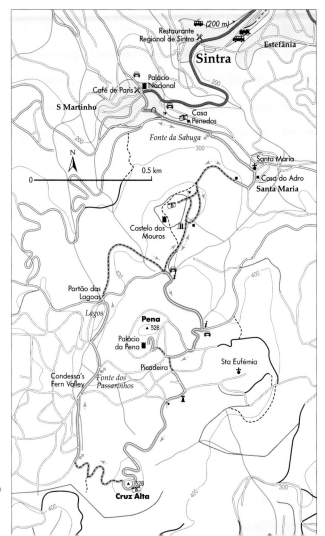

Wherever you are in Sintra, you will see signs of its historical popularity with monarchs and nobility as a place of retreat from the summer heat of Lisbon. Apart from the grand 'formal' palaces there are many smaller *palacetes* and follies dotted around the hillside, many with quite exquisite architecture, some quite bizarre!

Sintra was also a favourite with many well known names, including Hans Christian Andersen, Graham Greene, Richard Strauss, William Beckford and Lord Byron.

Byron first arrived in Lisbon by sea in July 1809:

'What beauties doth Lisboa first unfold!

Her image floating on that noble tide.'

Just two verses after the above lines in Childe Harold, he penned the following immortal words:

Lo! Cintra's glorious Eden intervenes

In variegated maze of mount and glen.

Ah, me! What hand can pencil guide, or pen,

To follow half on which the eye dilates

Through views more dazzling unto mortal ken

Although some 200 years have passed, there is enough of that original ambience and attraction today. It's well worth spending time in the old town (preferably avoiding the busy weekends), which is full of cafés, restaurants and shops offering antiques and handicrafts. But always above you are the hills, and atop the hills the Moors' Castle and Pena Palace. Even at night their floodlit presence is felt, often mysteriously wrapped in fast-moving mist or fog.

Begin the walk in the main square (**Largo do Palácio National de Sintra**) opposite the Café Paris Restaurant (179m). Walk up Rua das Padarias and, on the first bend, take steps up left to the **Arca Ferreirinha**. Once through this arch, turn right up more steps, following yellow and red waymarks and coming to signposts for PR1 and PR3 (**2min**). Turn left following the PR1 sign towards 'Igreja Santa Maria'. Pass the **Casa Penedos** on your left (from where there are fine views down to the National Palace) and come to the **Fonte da Sabuga** on your right (**5min**; being restored at the time of writing). Turn up right on cobbles (Calcada dos Clérigos) to the **Igreja Santa Maria** (**9min**). From the church walk up past **Casa do Adro** (where Hans Christian Andersen stayed in 1866) and, a minute later,

The path levels out as you walk below the Moors' Castle (18min)

turn right up the steep **Rampa do Castelo** (ignoring the 'X' way-mark), passing the **Forestry Department office** on the right.

The Lagos

The cobbles give way to steps and a dirt track which brings you to a narrow revolving gate — the entrance to the grounds surrounding the Moors' Castle (**13min**). Zigzag up to the right just 10 metres above the gate and, ignoring the steps up to the right (**18min**), follow the main, level path. But a minute later *do* fork right uphill (above a small castellated house). When the path swings round to the right (**20min**), ignore steps off to the left. A minute later, turn sharp left at a junction with a blue 'P' sign (the way ahead leads to the Moors' Castle, but first you need an entrance ticket). You immediately pass the old **grain silos** on your right. Walk through another revolving gate (**24min**) to the **Visitor Centre**. Here you should buy tickets to enter the Moors' Castle (on your return) and Pena Palace gardens (as well as the palace itself, if you wish to go inside). Turn left along the road past the Visitor Centre (signed to 'Palácio') and descend to a car park and another **Visitor Centre** (**28min**). Turn in through the gates (showing your ticket) and follow a well-marked road up to **Pena Palace** (487m; **40min**).

Pena Palace

After visiting the palace, return down to the pill-box just a minute below and turn left down a tarmac road. In two minutes turn right, to come to the open space at **Picadeira** (**44min**). Walk through this open space to the opposite corner and take the footpath up to the left (ignoring the tarmac road ahead under a bridge). In another half minute you rise to a rough tarmac-surfaced track; turn left and in another half minute fork right, to walk below the **Statue of the Giant**, perched on rocks. Walk round to the right of the statue, then turn left at the major junction (**47min**), coming immediately to a sign for 'Cruz Alta'.

Wind up the road to **Cruz Alta** (528m; **57min**). Where the road divides, just below the summit, keep left, then take the steps up to the viewpoint. Return down the same steps and, when you rejoin the tarred surface, turn right. You pass another flight of steps lead down from the viewpoint (**59min**): opposite these steps, go through a break in the wall on the left, to find a couple more steps leading down to a steep narrow footpath.

Follow this down through dense woodland and, at a junction (**1h10min**) keep right downhill. At the next, T-junction, turn right (**1h14min**). In another minute you will come down to a **fountain and water tank**, just beyond which you join a dirt trail. Turn right here, now on the level. At a junction with two trails off left (**1h21min**), take the second one, going steeply downhill for a minute, to a tarmac road. Cross the road and walk into the **Condessa's Fern Valley**. Various paths lead down through this beautiful verdant valley; it doesn't matter which one you take — just keep downhill. In

Sintra National Palace with twin chimneys rising above the kitchens

three minutes you come out onto tarmac again, where you turn right to the Moorish **Fonte das Passarinhos**.

On leaving this fountain, walk down left on tarmac, following the 'Lagos' sign. At the **Lagos** (lakes; **1h26min**) look out for the resident black swans and grey herons as you continue downhill, now following signs to the **Portão das Lagoas** (gateway; **1h28min**). Cross the main road up to the right and go through the gate opposite (by a blue 'P' sign). Follow the trail, then path, round and below **Pena Palace** to emerge back at the **Visitor Centre** (**1h37min**). Retrace your outward route to the first junction with the blue 'P' sign and now keep ahead to

a junction, where you turn left up to the entrance to the **Castelo dos Mouros** (Moors' Castle; 435m; **1h42min**). Show your ticket, walk through the gate and explore the grounds inside the castle walls. There are spectacular views down to Sintra and back to Pena Palace, as well as the coast beyond — on clear days.

On leaving the castle, retrace your steps to the T-junction just below the entrance, where you follow the sign for the GR11 footpath. This will bring you back down to the 18min-point of the outward route in six minutes. Retrace your steps back down to the old centre of **Sintra** (**2h06min**, *not including* visits!).

Queijadas de Sintra

Many Portuguese towns have their own 'speciality' cake. Sintra is no exception, and the *queijadas de Sintra* (Sintra cheesecakes) have a fame which goes well beyond the town itself.

Like most Portuguese pastries, they are quite sweet, the ingredients being soft sheep's milk cheese, sugar, flour, eggs and cinnamon.

Several shops sell *queijadas*, but the most famous are probably those sold at the always-busy **Piriquita** bakery — just across the road from Café de Paris (by the start of this walk).

Sintra is a very popular attraction for visitors the whole year round, its proximity to Lisbon and its World Heritage status providing good reasons for a day out from the capital. Not surprisingly, a vigorous hotel and restaurant trade has developed in response to tourist demands. In fact you can eat out in splendour at Queluz National Palace, stay overnight in the Seteais Palace or choose from many other excellent hotels and restaurants in and around the town.

We have selected just a couple of restaurants, one for this walk and another for Walk 3, but do not regard our choice as in any way exclusive!

For this walk we have chosen the small **Restaurante Regional de Sintra**, a restaurant tucked away behind the Sintra Town Hall, halfway between the old centre and the railway station. The staff are very helpful and friendly, and the restaurant is pleasantly decorated with tile murals (see overleaf). The menu is available in English.

RESTAURANTE REGIONAL DE SINTRA
Travessa do Município 1, Sintra
℡/fax 219 234 444
Daily €€

good choice of **starters**, including several traditional soups, like *canja* (chicken broth), *açorda à Alentejana* (coriander soup with poached egg; recipe on page 45).

plenty of **fish and seafood** dishes, choose either plain grilled fish or try a *caldeirada de mariscos* (seafood stew) or *caril de gambas* (prawn curry; recipe on page 44).

meat dishes include steaks done in several different ways, pork, chicken and lamb

for **sweets** there is an ice-cream menu and home-made dishes including chocolate mousse, Molotov pudding (a creation of beaten egg whites with a rich egg yolk sauce) or a selection of fresh fruit.

restaurants

eat

Goan-style curry *(caril de gambas)*

Wash the prawns and cook them in salted boiling water for 2 minutes. Drain and cool in cold water, then remove the heads and shells.

Heat the butter in a saucepan, add chopped onion, apple and pineapple and cook until soft. Stir in the flour until well blended, then add the curry powder and cook for a few minutes. Gradually stir in the coconut milk and milk, add seasoning as required and bring to the boil.

Lower the heat and cook for 15-20 minutes, stirring occasionally. If the mixture becomes too thick, add a little more milk. Remove from the heat, cool, then put the mixture in a blender until smooth. Return the blended ingredients to the saucepan, add the peeled and shelled prawns and heat through.

Serve on a bed of plain boiled rice, sprinkle the prawns with desiccated coconut, and garnish with slices of fresh fruit — perhaps apple, banana, kiwi and grapes.

Ingredients (for 4 people)

1 kg raw prawns
1 onion, chopped
1 apple, chopped
2 pineapple rings, chopped
1 tbsp flour
1 tbsp curry powder
50 g butter
200 ml coconut milk
400 ml milk
salt and pepper
desiccated coconut
fresh fruit to garnish

recipes

eat

Coriander soup with poached egg *(açorda à Alentejana)*

Crush the garlic cloves with the salt using a pestle and mortar. Add the finely chopped coriander and put into the bottom of a serving bowl with the olive oil.

In the meantime, poach the eggs in the water and, when cooked, remove them. Then add the boiling water to the crushed ingredients, together with some of the bread and mix well. Tear the rest of the bread into pieces and add to the mixture. Use as much or as little bread as you wish.

Put the poached eggs on top of the soup and serve, each serving containing a poached egg.

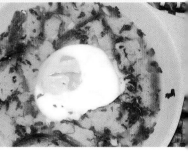

Restaurante Regional de Sintra: their versions of Goan-style curry and coriander soup, and one of the tile murals depicting the town.

Ingredients (for 4 people)

4 eggs
2 garlic cloves
1 tbsp sea salt
4 tbsp olive oil
1.5 l boiling water
400 g day-old bread
4 tbsp coriander

This walk links the botanical gardens and Palace of Monserrate with the fascinating Capuchos Convent via the woods above Monserrate. The convent is a truly remarkable contrast to the spacious splendour and beauty of Monserrate's gardens — the two extremes separated by some pleasant woodland walking.

monserrate and capuchos

WALK

Start the walk at the car park by the **Visitor Centre** opposite the entrance to **Monserrate Gardens** (208m). Walk through the small gate behind the centre, past a water tank and fountain, rising on a footpath over gnarled old tree roots. This takes you up to a **pond with water lilies** on your left. Carry on round to the left as you join a track above the pond, passing a **concrete building** on your right (**3min**). At a crossroads (**6min**) continue straight ahead; do the same a minute later, climbing steadily.

After reaching the top of the rise, ignore the first right turn and take the *next* right turn (**10min**), heading downhill and passing a small **pond**

Distance: 6km/3.7mi; 1h20min

Grade: easy-moderate, with some moderate uphill stretches and 150m height gain (490ft), but always good underfoot, on forestry tracks. *IGE 1:25,000 M888 Series map, sheets 415 and 416*

Equipment: see pages 14-15

Transport: 🚂 from Lisbon to Sintra (very frequent; see page 142), then taxi from the railway station to Monserrate (4km). Or 🚗 to Monserrate

Refreshments:
Only at Sintra; nothing en route

Opening times/Prices
Convento dos Capuchos daily for guided visits; first at 10.00, last at 16.30; €3.50
Monserrate Palace daily for guided visits at 10.00 and 15.00 (*must be booked in advance:* ☎ 219 237 300); €7.00 (includes the **gardens**). Palace **gardens** only: daily 09.30-18.00 (last admissions 17.00); €3.50 each

on the left (**12min**). Keep ahead as a track joins from the left a minute later. You emerge at what appears to be a T-junction (**20min**), but is in fact a crossroads of tracks (there is a lesser grassy track ahead). Turn left here, in another two minutes coming to a large old **reservoir**. Walk round to the left of the

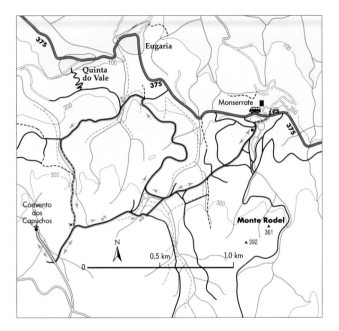

reservoir and, at the far side, take the turning up left on another motorable track.

This dirt road leads you uphill until you come to a T-junction on a curve (**26min**), where you turn left. At a fork (**35min**) keep ahead, now walking on the level. You will come to a T-junction (358m; **41min**), with a sign indicating the **perimeter of the Serra de Sintra Forest**. Turn right here to visit the **Convento de Capuchos** (**49min**) — but note that you will return to this junction for the return leg of the walk, which is to the left.

After visiting the convent retrace your steps to the T-junction (**57min**) and continue ahead. Pass a **water storage tank** on your left (it has a small *azulejo* panel with the date 1888 on the far wall) and start downhill. Bear right at the three-way junction (**1h**). In just under two minutes keep ahead at a fork, passing a new **reservoir** on the right (**1h05min**) and ignoring another track joining from the right half a minute later.

Winding downhill through the woods on this main forestry track, you come to a junction where you carry

The Convento dos Capuchos was founded in 1590 and provides a stark contrast to the splendour of Monserrate.

The tiny monastery is located in the midst of a jumble of huge rocks and boulders and takes austerity to the limit. The individual cells, sufficient for a dozen inmates, are built into the rock, the only insulation provided by cork lining the doors and ceilings. Beds were simply cork bark laid out on the floor.

A guided visit is a fascinating way to learn about the layout and functionality of this hideaway — and about the harsh life and discipline of the monks.

on straight ahead (**1h11min**; the left turn here was taken on the outward route). Ignore the trail off right two minutes later, and retrace your steps back down past the concrete building above the lily pond, to the **Visitor Centre** (**1h20min**). You can buy a ticket here to visit the gardens of Monserrate.

Monserrate Park: the gardens and park have existed since the end of the 18th century, from which time various owners and tenants have attempted to create a botanical garden.

The writer William Beckford rented the property from 1794 and created, amongst other things, the waterfall just inside the entrance. However, most influential of all in the development of the park was Sir Francis Cook (1st Viscount of Monserrate), who acquired the property in 1856. Apart from extensive landscaping and planting, he engaged the English architect James Knowles, together with a thousand workers to create the neo-oriental palace (the exterior of which has recently been restored).

The artist William Stockdale was also involved at the time in developing the botanical gardens. In 1949 ownership passed to the Portuguese State and, after some decades of relative neglect, the park and buildings are now the subject of extensive restoration work which is expected to continue for some years.

Café de Paris

This well known restaurant is just in front of the National Palace. Sitting on the esplanade, watching the horse and carriage drive past, takes you back to the romantic era of the 19th

> **CAFE DE PARIS**
> **Praça a República, 32, Sintra**
> (**219 232 375/fax 219 255 519**
> **daily** €€€
>
> **light meals** including **sandwiches**, **salads** and **omelettes**
>
> **starters** include *melão com presunto* (melon with smoked ham), soups, prawns done in various ways and the 'Chef's starter': *carapaus de escabeche* (marinated horse-mackerel; recipe on page 53).
>
> grilled **fish** and **combination fish and seafood** dishes based on traditional recipes, like *arroz de marisco* (seafood rice) and *açorda do marisco* (seafood mixed with bread, coriander and egg).
>
> the **house speciality** is *naco ao sal* (tornedo steak cooked entirely in a case of salt), but there are other steak dishes. We also recommend *peito de frango recheado com espinafres e nozes* (chicken breast stuffed with spinach and nuts; recipe on page 52) and the *cabrito à moda de colares* (roast kid Colares-style, served with a very rich gravy).
>
> **sweets** include ice-cream, fresh fruit and offers from the trolley

century. If you eat indoors, look at the lovely painted ceiling. Good service, well-presented meals, and a reasonably-priced Tourist Menu. Unlike some of the other 'touristy' restaurants in Sintra, the Café de Paris usually has some authentic Portuguese dishes on offer.

restaurants

eat

Chicken breast stuffed with spinach and nuts
(peito de frango recheado com espinafres e nozes)

Make a pocket in each of the 4 chicken breasts, season with salt, pepper and lemon juice.

Mix the nuts and chopped spinach together and stuff the chicken breasts with the mixture, then secure with skewers.

Heat the butter in a frying pan, but do not let it burn. Add the chicken breasts, turning down the heat and gently fry, turning occasionally, until cooked.

Top with the sauce and serve with plain boiled rice.

Ingredients (for 4 people)
4 chicken breasts
1 cup of lightly boiled, well drained, spinach
20 g nuts (chopped walnuts, almonds or pine nuts)
1 lemon
2 tbsp butter
salt and pepper

For the sauce
600 ml basic white sauce
1 tbsp cream
1 tsp curry powder

Chicken with spinach and nuts at the Café de Paris, with extra spinach served in a wine glass. Opposite: the restaurant's presentation of the carapaus and a general display

recipes

eat

Marinated horse-mackerel (carapaus de escabeche)

Horse-mackerel are small, sardine-like fish so, if you make the recipe back home, use small sardines.

Clean and dry the *carapaus*, dip in flour, shake off surplus then fry in hot olive oil until slightly browned. Place in a glass or ceramic dish with a lid.

To prepare the marinade: Simmer all the ingredients in a covered saucepan for 15 minutes, then pour the mixture over the fish. Cover and leave to marinate for 3 days in the refrigerator. Serve cold.

Ingredients (for 4 people)
1 kg *carapaus* (or small sardines)
flour
olive oil
for the marinade
100 ml white vinegar
300 ml dry white wine
100 ml water
1 tsp salt
pepper
2 carrots, grated
2 onions, sliced
2 cloves garlic, finely chopped
1 tbsp chopped parsley
100 ml olive oil
1 bay leaf

Perched at 487m atop the westernmost summit of the Sintra Hills, Peninha Chapel provides wonderful views out to Cabo da Roca, Guincho Beach and the Cascais-Estoril coast. Legend has it that at this spot the Virgin Mary appeared as a beautiful girl before a mute shepherdess and gave her speech.

peninha circuit from azóia

WALK

To commemorate this miracle, a humble chapel was built in thanks to the Virgin. The present chapel and surrounding buildings date back to 1753 and now have a somewhat austere and abandoned aspect. The place can get very busy at weekends, as it is possible to drive very nearly to the top. This should not detract from the walk which, although a fairly stiff climb up, keeps well away from roads and passes through some varied scenery. The main walk up is mostly through woodland, so you

Distance: 5.6km/3.5mi; 1h20min

Grade: easy-moderate; there is an height gain of 220m (720ft). Much of the walk is on good forestry tracks, although the main ascent is on a steep woodland footpath. *IGE 1:25,000 M888 Series map, sheet 415*

Equipment: see pages 14-15

Transport: 🚌 from Sintra station; there is a regular Scott URB service (bus 403; timetable page 142) that will take you to Azóia junction; journey time is about 40 minutes. This same service goes through to Cascais, from where you can also catch a 🚈 into Lisbon. Or 🚗 to/from Azóia

Refreshments: restaurants and cafés Azóia; *nothing en route*

will do the hard work in the shade; the return downhill is on the sparsely-vegetated southwest face of the Sintra range, which provides a remarkable contrast to the luxuriant vegetation seen everywhere else in these hills.

Start the walk at the **road junction above Azóia** (where the EN247-4 to Cabo Roca leaves the main EN247). There is a bus stop here or, if you have come by car, just 25m down the EN247-4 towards Azóia you will find an **information post** with space alongside for **parking** (altitude 266m).

From the **bus stop** walk 25m along the road (towards

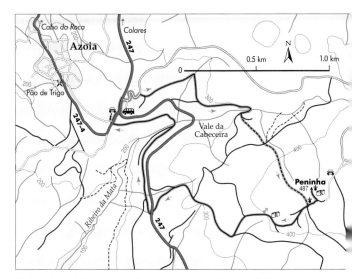

Colares) and then turn right up the tarred road, following the **blue sign posts** to Monserrate and Peninha. You will come to a **metal canopy** structure behind a fence, on a sharp left-hand bend (**4min**). Turn right on the dirt road immediately after the canopy and, immediately after, bear round to the left (where a lesser dirt track comes in from the right); there is a white SMAS water supply **concrete valve housing** on the left. Continue on the level along this forestry track, passing another SMAS valve housing on the left (**7min**). The track swings round to the right (**10min**), crosses a small watercourse and soon begins to rise. On another right hand bend (**17min**), be sure to bear left at the fork. Two minutes later the track swings round to the left; on the outside of this bend, take the path leading steeply up to the right, into the pine woods.

The spreading heads of cypresses (*Cupressus lusitanica*) form a dense canopy along this path, under which little else but the carpet of ivy can grow. Cross straight over an earthen trail (**23min**) and follow the path up the hill ahead. You emerge at the top of the woods, by a **blocked gateway** in an old stone wall (**30min**). Turn right and immediately left through a gap in the wall, following the footpath beyond it. You now get extensive views out over the coast and back to the mouth of the Tagus.

The path leads up below spreading cypresses, through a carpet of ground ivy

On joining a dirt track, turn left uphill. You pass a ruined chapel and arrive at the wall below Peninha (**33min**). As you rise to approach this wall, turn sharp left, onto another track just above, now continuing just below the wall. This leads you immediately to some steps which give access to the walled-in area of the main chapel and buildings of **Peninha Chapel** (487m; **35min**).

Hazy-day view from Peninha to Cabo da Roca

After taking in the fabulous views, retrace your steps down to the ruined chapel (**38min**). Turn left on the wide dirt track leading downhill just past this and, almost immediately, take the right-hand fork, following another dirt track downhill. Look out along here for pale pink to white sea pinks (*Armeria pseudo-armeria*) and the shrubby pimpernel, *Anagellis moneli*, with its small clear blue flowers. Carry on round to the right where another dirt road comes in from the left and in another minute you will see Cabo da Roca in the distance.

After passing a **water pumping station** on the right (**43min**), turn left at a junction (**46min**). You pass some shrubs that look suspiciously like *Grevillea* that must have 'escaped' from one of Sintra's formal gardens. At the next major T-junction of tracks, turn right downhill, emerging at an old gateway (**52min**). Walk through, turn left and, one minute later, at another T-junction, turn left again. This dirt track takes you down to the main EN247 road (**1h04min**).

Cross the road, turn left, and after 20m take the dirt road off right, which you follow parallel to and below the main road. Continue straight ahead at a fork (**1h06min**) and cross a **stream** (**1h13min**), beyond which the dirt road rises steadily up to Azóia. When you come out on the EN247-4, turn right; the **car park** is just 20m up the road, the **bus stop and starting point** just beyond this (**1h20min**).

There are several restaurants in Azóia, popular with visitors on their way to or from Cabo da Roca. We confess to choosing Pão de Trigo somewhat at random and were not disappointed!

Pão de Trigo

You're likely to be welcomed with the selection of *petiscos* shown below — olives, *presunto* (smoked ham), a *saloio* (cows') cheese, locally-baked bread and butter. Tip: we found the local Colares red wine served here, Casal da Azenha, good value.

PÃO DE TRIGO
Estrada do Cabo da Rocha, Azóia
(219 290 850/fax 219 280 181
daily except Thursdays €€

varied menu with **omelettes** and **salads** for a light meal

specialities include *robalo* (bass), *sargo* (sea-bream) and *linguado* (sole) freshly caught from the Cabo da Roca, as well as *espetadas* (kebabs) of fish and meat

grilled sardines in summer

seafood also features very prominently — including *camarão* (prawns), *percebes* (barnacles) and *amêijoas* (cockles)

meat dishes include the mixed meat kebab, steak au poivre or 'steak a café', grilled chicken, roast kid, pork chops and escalopes of beef with mushroom in a Madeira sauce

plenty of choice for **sweets**, including fresh fruit, both local and exotic, chocolate mousse, sweet rice (recipe page 103), rum baba, ice-cream and many more

restaurants

eat

Turbot and prawn kebab *(espetada de peixe com camarão)*

Preheat the grill to moderate while you assemble the kebabs. Cut each fillet of turbot into 6 pieces and thread onto a skewer, alternating with the red and green peppers, the onion and the prawns.

Preparing the kebabs at home

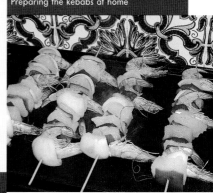

Brush the kebabs with olive oil and cook them on the grill, turning them every 2 minutes until they are cooked.

Serve with boiled potatoes, carrots, beans and broccoli (or any vegetables that are in season) and a small dish of tartar sauce.

Restaurante Pão de Trigo

Ingredients (for 4 people)
4 thick fillets of turbot (or any other chunky, firm white fish)
12 squares of green pepper
12 squares of red pepper
2 large onions
12 raw prawns
2 tbsp olive oil
4 skewers

recipes

eat

The coast west of Colares has long attracted summer visitors from Sintra, as an alternative to Lisbon's Cascais and Estoril beaches. Indeed, so popular was this route to the sea that a 12km-long tramline *(eléctrico)* was built all the way from Sintra to Praia das Maçãs. In summer you can use this practical route to start the walk.

azenhas do mar

WALK

Start the walk at Várzea de Colares, at the junction with the road to Praia das Maçãs. The *eléctrico* stops just one minute away from this junction, opposite the Adega Cooperativa.

Set off along the right-hand side of the road, crossing the **Ribeira de Colares** and then passing the **Colares Wine Co-operative** on the right. Keep on the main road past the turn-off right to Mucifal (**4min**), but then turn right on a narrow surfaced road (Rua de Brancaflor; **6min**). This road soon reverts to track. Continue ahead, bearing right at a fork (**9min**). You pass through a belt of summer homes on either side of the track and then come back onto tarmac for a short stretch; keep straight on where a tarmac lane comes in from the left (**11min**), after which the tarmac ceases.

Distance: 10.8km/6.7mi; 2h11min

Grade: easy, generally over level ground and good underfoot on tracks and lanes. *IGE 1:25,000 M888 Series map, sheet 415*

Equipment: see pages 14-15

Transport: Scott URB 🚌 403 or 441 from Sintra station to Várzea de Colares; same bus to return (timetables on page 142). 🚋 From June to September you can take the tram mentioned opposite, a journey of about 50 minutes; board it near Sintra station. Trams run every hour all the way to Praia das Maçãs. Or 🚗 to/from Várzea de Colares

Refreshments en route:
Restaurants, bars/cafés at Várzea de Colares, Azenhas do Mar, Praia Grande, Praia das Maçãs

Sintra tram *(eléctrico)*; in summer you can take it all the way to Praia das Maçãs

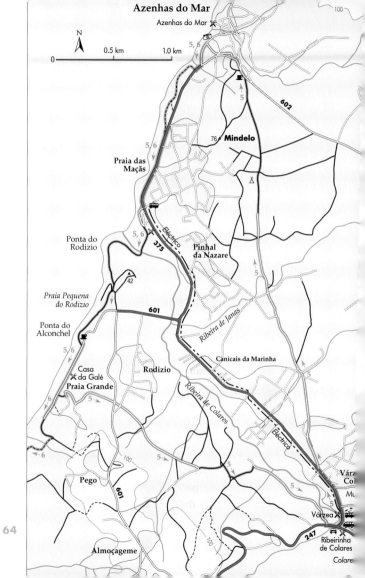

Ducks in the river at Várzea de Colares

Ignoring all side turnings, continue straight on — first across a small **stream** (**24min**) and then across another track (**29min**). Soon after passing a **caravan site** on the left, some vineyards come into view. These have nylon netting windbreaks (instead of the traditional bamboo canes) and are not very extensive. Wine production in the Colares region is under ever-increasing pressure from property developers. Keep ahead past the vineyards, join a track coming in from the left (**42min**) and soon come to the outskirts of Azenhas do Mar.

Turn left at the tarmac road in front of the café Adega das Azenhas (**44min**) and pass the small bandstand on the right.

Fisherman perched atop the cliffs near Azenhas do Mar

This takes you into the upper square of **Azenhas do Mar** (**47min**). There are shops and a couple of bars where you can have some refreshments.

From the square, take the cobbled road (Azinhaga do Beiriz) down to the main **Praia das Maças road** (**49min**). Cross over and turn right to a viewpoint *(miradouro)* from where you can photograph the spectacular cliff scenery and the old houses of Azenhas do Mar clinging to the rockface of the headland to the north (photograph page 62).

From the *miradouro* walk south on the main road, then turn right at the 'Velocidade Controlada' sign (**50min**; there is a red and white waymark). From here you can walk along the cliff tops towards Praia das Maças for a while. The scenery is spectacular, and you will doubtless see fishermen perched on the cliff top, casting their lines into the heaving swell 40m below. Eventually private properties block the way along the cliff, and you are forced to rejoin the main road (**58min**). Follow the road into **Praia das Maças**, taking the fork down right to the **beach** (**1h07min**).

Just by the beach-front restaurants (Loureiro and Neptune) you will see red and white waymarks and a signpost for the GR11. Walk out across the beach towards the low cliff opposite. You will need to cross the stream (**1h10min**) at its narrowest point, just in front of the headland. If there has been very heavy rain (occasionally possible in the winter) it can be *dangerous* to try crossing here.*

Climb up the lower ramp, close to the sea (alternatively, climb up a little way back from the cliff edge), to reach the **top**

---

*In this case you should *retrace your steps to the village* and then follow the main road out towards Colares. Turn right in 10 minutes by the sign to 'Praia Grande' and immediately cross the stream on the road. You can now either just follow the road up the hill and then down into Praia Grande (rejoining the main walk in 15 minutes), or turn right immediately after the bridge and follow the track that runs alongside the stream back out to the headland.

Traditional viniculture north of Azenhas do Mar, with cane windbreaks

of the headland (**1h13min**). Then follow the sandy track along the cliff top. Keep ahead, ignoring the track down to Rodizio Beach (**1h19min**), soon passing a café and restaurant on the left. Praia Grande comes into view ahead, and you join the tarmac road leading to it.

Walk down the road and along the front, until you come to a small roundabout in front of the Casa da Galé Restaurant (see Walk 6, pages 82-83; **1h30min**). Continue ahead until the white wall on your left ends, then follow a track uphill to the left. On coming to a T-junction (**1h33min**), turn left. Walk along the track, parallel with the shore below.

Restaurante Casa da Galé (see pages 82-83)

You pass through a residential area, then curve up right to another T-junction (**1h38min**), where you turn left, now on tarmac. This lane climbs steadily and swings round to the right; soon, as you crest the rise, Pena Palace appears in the distance.

When you reach a main road (**1h43min**), cross over and keep straight on at the crossroads immediately after, continuing downhill along the lane ahead. This tarmac-surfaced lane will take you down through attractive mixed pine and mimosa woods. You pass a turning left (Rua das Areias), after which the lane begins to level out. Ignore a track off right (**1h53min**), but turn right into Rua Mesquita at a crossroads a minute later (where a dirt track straight ahead leads to a water treatment plant). Take the next left turn two minutes later (still on Rua Mesquita), to continue through an area of market gardens. Coming on to a tarred surface once more (**2h07min**), turn left on reaching the main road (**2h10min**) at **Várzea de Colares**. Walk back downhill for one minute, to the junction where the walk began.

There are a couple of good restaurants in Várzea de Colares (and even more if you are prepared to walk up the hill to Colares village itself). We came to thoroughly enjoy the Ribeirinha de Colares — for all the right reasons: good food, a pleasant, 'warm' ambience, and very helpful staff.

Ribeirinha de Colares

This restaurant specialises in meals that reflect traditional Portuguese flavours. The menu, which varies daily, is very tempting, and it is always difficult to choose between the imaginative dishes on offer.

There is also a delicatessen and grocery shop where you can find Portuguese cheeses, pâtés, smoked ham and other Portuguese and foreign products. Some of the finest Portuguese wines, including, of course, a selection of the famous Colares

Dining room at Ribeirinha de Colares

restaurants

eat

RESTAURANTE DA VÁRZEA
Largo Infante D. Henriques, 8,
Colares (219 280 212
daily except Tuesdays
€-€€

wide selection of excellent **pizzas** and **salads** for a light meal

main courses include grilled **steak**, **fish** and **chicken** dishes

RIBEIRINHA DE COLARES
Av Bombeiros Voluntários, 71,
Colares (219 282 175
www.ribeirinha_colares.pt
daily except Mondays, from 10am
€€

coffee and **light snacks** all day; wide range of **traditional meals**

entradas include olives, local cheese and *pão caseiro* (freshly baked country-style bread), served with *flor do olival* (a very fine olive oil, in which you dip the bread)

AZENHAS DO MAR
Piscinas das Azenhas do Mar
Tel: 219 280 739
Open every day €€
Multibanco debit cards only

specialises in charcoal-grilled fresh fish and seafood (the price of the fish depends on the weight, so always ask the price before ordering — or you may have a bit of a shock!)

other **seafood** offerings include *caril de gambas* (prawn curry; recipe page 44) and *polvo assado* (roast octopus)

meat dishes include pork, roast beef and duck.

reds, are to be found in the wine section.

Another very good restaurant in Várzea de Colares, slightly less sophisticated, but with good wholesome food and a friendly atmosphere is just over the road from Ribeirinha de Colares, alongside the bridge: the **Restaurante da Várzea**. You can enjoy your meal here sitting on the esplanade. In summer there is live music.

The spectacularly-located **Restaurante Azenhas do Mar**, clinging to th cliffs alongside the swimming pool at Azenhas do Mar (with a lovely patio), is another good option.

Rabbit stew (ensopado de coelho à Alentejano)

Fry the chopped onions, crushed garlic and rabbit portions all together in the olive oil until the rabbit has turned brown. Then add the stock, red

wine and bay leaf. Season with salt and pepper.

Bring to the boil and cook gently for about 3-4 minutes, then add the quartered potatoes. Bring to the boil again. Cover and simmer until the rabbit and potatoes are cooked (about 20-30 minutes).

Place the fried bread in 4 deep serving dishes and cover with rabbit portions. Spoon the potatoes around the bread and rabbit and pour the juice over. Garnish with chopped parsley.

This dish (shown here as served at the Ribeirinha de Colares restaurant) is a cross between a soup and a stew. The *pão caseiro* they use is baked locally.

<u>Ingredients (for 4 people)</u>
1 rabbit, jointed
2 onions, finely chopped
2 garlic cloves, crushed
2 tbsp olive oil
200 ml stock
300 ml red wine (preferably the local Colares)
0.5 kg potatoes
1 bay leaf
salt and pepper
chopped parsley, to garnish
4 thick slices of fried *pão caseiro* (or a dense, day-old bread)

recipes

eat

Prawn bread soup (açorda de camarão)

Like the rabbit dish opposite, this is a cross between a soup and a stew. Cook the prawns in salted boiling water for 2 minutes. Drain and keep the water. Cool the prawns, shell them and remove the heads. Return the heads and shells to the cooking water and boil uncovered for about 10 minutes, or until the liquid has reduced a little.

Pour 600 ml of this liquid over the bread, reserving the rest of the liquid — or use pre-prepared fish stock from a stock cube.

Fry the chopped garlic in the olive oil, then add the soaked bread, stirring until you have a soft, mushy consistency. Season with salt, pepper and a dash of piri-piri. Add the prawns and the finely chopped coriander and heat through.

If the soup is too dry, add some of the reserved cooking water. Finally, add the well-beaten eggs and cook, stirring gently, for 2 to 3 minutes. Check seasoning before serving.

Ingredients (for 4 people)
1 kg prawns
500 g day-old bread
3 cloves of garlic
4 eggs, well beaten
4 tbsp olive oil
600 ml stock (fish stock cube or water in which the prawns have been cooked; a glass of white wine could be included in the total liquid)
4 tbsp fresh coriander
salt and pepper
piri-piri (see page 140)

Cabo da Roca, the westernmost point of mainland Europe, is the final goal of this walk, and you can even get a certificate to prove you've been there! But even if you don't go the whole way, you will see some wonder-fully dramatic coastal scenery, bird life and wild flowers — all with bracing sea air and the roar of the ocean!

westward to cabo da roca

WALK

Start the walk at **Praia das Maçãs**. Just by the beach-front restaurants (Loureiro and Neptune) you will see red and white waymarks and a signpost for the GR11. Walk out across the beach towards the low cliff opposite. You will need to cross the stream (**3min**) at its narrowest point, just in front of the headland. If there has been very heavy rain (occasionally possible in the winter) it can be *dangerous* to try crossing here. Should this be the case, refer to the footnote on page 67.

Climb up the lower ramp, close to the sea (alternatively, climb up a little way back from the cliff edge), to reach the **top of the headland** (**6min**). A sandy track leads you along the cliff top, where the invasive Hottentott fig, *Caprobutus edulis*, with its succulent leaves and large yellow flowers, is much in

Distance: 9.7km/6mi; 2h52min (one way)

Grade: moderate. There are some steep gradients from the beaches up onto the cliff tops involving two 80m climbs each way (265ft); otherwise the walk is fairly easy going. Most of the route is waymarked (red and white for the GR11). *IGE 1:25,000 M888 Series map, sheet 415*

Equipment: see pages 14-15

Transport: Scott URB 🚌 441 from Sintra station to Praia das Maçãs (journey time about 25 minutes). Or take the 🚌 from Sintra (see pages 62-63). Return from Cabo da Roca on Scott URB 🚌 403 — either back to Sintra station (journey time 45 minutes) or to Cascais (30 minutes), from where you can catch a 🚆 to Lisbon. Timetable information on page 142

Shorter version: 🚐 If you have your own transport, you could do an out-and-back walk from Praia Grande (14km/8.7mi; 4h17min)

Refreshments en route:
Bars, cafés and restaurants at Praia das Maçãs, Praia Grande, Praia da Adraga, Cabo da Roca and nearby Azóia (see page 60)

Praia Grande, from the trig point reached in 40min

evidence. Keep ahead, ignoring the track down to Rodizio Beach (**12min**), soon passing a café and restaurant on the left. Praia Grande comes into view ahead, and you join the tarmac road leading to it (**15min**). Walk down the road and along the front until you come to a small roundabout in front of the Casa da Galé Restaurant (**23min**; see page 82). Even if you're not ready for lunch, do take a break here.

Then continue ahead, down the ramp and onto the sand. There seems to be no continuation off the beach, but in just a couple of minutes you will see another red and white waymark on a boulder ahead, indicating the way to the bottom of a stairway up to the cliff top. Climb the steps — all 320 of them — and, once at the top (**34min**), turn sharp right, following the

Pistacia lentiscus (top) and the old lime kiln at Praia da Adraga

waymarks out to the **trig point** (71m; **40min**). You will certainly want to pause here, to recuperate from the climb and take in the particularly fine view to the north over the great expanse of Praia Grande (photograph on page 77).

Heading on from here, navigation is very easy, as you are following part of the GR11 route. The red and white waymarks guide you across the cliff top towards Praia da Adraga. The joints in the limestone surface have weathered here to a karst pavement, where the larger cracks and fissures are filled with windblown sand or in some cases provide shelter for vegetation and flowers such as sweet alison (*Lobularia maritima*).

Make sure you take the waymarked sharp left turn through the old derelict wall (**49min**). (The lesser path ahead, marked with an 'X', leads to a dangerous descent to Praia da Adraga.) The path now heads a short way inland, passing clumps of juniper (*Juniperus Phoenicia*), mastic (*Pistacia lentiscus*) and, in spring, colourful *Antirrhinum major*, before dropping down through mixed woodlands of mimosa, giant reeds, pines and eucalyptus and becoming sandy underfoot. The path turns down right and soon joins a major sandy trail (**54min**). Turn right here and walk into a stand of umbrella pines a minute later.

Walk down through these lovely trees and, when the path divides just below the trees, follow the waymarking down the left fork, to reach the road (**1h01min**). (Alternatively, if you wish to visit the café, the restaurant mentioned on page 82, or the toilets at **Praia da Adraga**, descend the right-hand path.)

Turn left along the road, away from Praia da Adraga and, a minute later, take the track off right (waymarked, and with a signpost 'Cabo da Roca 4.5km'). As the track takes you up a small valley, make sure you follow the waymarking sharply to the right (**1h07min**), then continue until you come to a T-junction at the **top of the valley** (**1h11min**). (*Ignore* the rough track off to the right one minute before reaching the T-junction; it is marked with an 'X', indicating 'wrong way'.)

At the T-junction the waymarking indicates that you should turn left, towards Cabo da Roca. However, rather than go directly there, it is well worth taking the *right turn* here and walking out to the cliffs. So turn right, and in two minutes you will come to another T-junction near the cliff top. Turn right again here and walk north for four minutes, to reach some impressive **caves and a blowhole** in the cliffs.

Retrace your steps to the cliff top T-junction (**1h21min**) and carry straight on along the cliffs, now heading south. The track crosses a fairly sharp little gully (**1h25min**) and rises onto the

Pedra de Alvidrar, seen from the point above Praia da Ursa

cliff top above **Praia da Ursa** (**1h35min**), with views on over to Cabo da Roca. Look out for kestrels *(Falco tinnunculus)* and Peregrine falcons *(Falco peregrinus)* too.

To your right and in front of the small beach is the islet-pinnacle called Pedra da Ursa (Bear Rock). Legend has it that this (female) bear defied the instructions of the gods to move north when the Sintra ice cap started to melt. As a punishment she was turned into stone, together with her cubs, which form the lesser rocks off the shore — including Pedra de Alvidrar shown here.

The scenery is magnificent. It is tempting to try to reach the cape by carrying on straight ahead, *but do not try!* There is no proper path ,and it is very steep and slippery. Instead, retrace your steps to the cliff top T-junction and turn right, back to the valley-top T-junction (**1h52min**). From here you have the choice of turning left and retracing your steps to Praia das Maçãs (3h03min), or turning right and carrying on to Cabo da Roca (2h52min).

To make for Cabo da Roca, turn right and follow the track as it winds inland (thereby avoiding the deep valley of the Ursa stream). Not far past a **ruined building** on the right (**1h55min**), you will see a small area of traditional viniculture on the left. The track reaches its highest point (124m; **1h58min**), then starts to drop quite steeply. It takes you to a junction, where you turn right (**2h08min**), as indicated by a waymarked rock on the right. Four minutes later, as the track is rising up a small slope, it divides, but both forks rejoin at the top, where you come to a T-junction (**1h13min**). Ignore the waymarked track off to the left here; follow the right-hand track signposted to Cabo da Roca.

Cross the **Ribeira da Ursa** (**2h16min**) and take the left fork just beyond it. Follow the track round to where another track joins from the left (**2h24min**) and up to a tarmac road (**2h29min**). Turn right here and follow the road out to **Cabo da Roca** (**2h52min**). The cape itself, at 9°30' west of Greenwich, is the westernmost extremity of mainland Europe. A monument with a plaque explains this and quotes Luís Camões, Portugal's great poet: 'Here … where the land ends and the sea begins …' — a fitting reminder of the crucial role played by the Portuguese in discovering and opening up the trade routes of the world some 500 years ago.

Just inland from the monument there is a bar, restaurant and toilets. There is also a **tourist information office**, where you can obtain a certificate confirming your visit to the far west of Europe. From here you can either catch a bus to Cascais (then train to Lisbon), or retrace your steps to Praia das Maçãs (reached in another 2h11min, making a total of just over 5h).

Casa da Galé

This restaurant (photograph on page 69) overlooks the huge expanse of beautiful Praia Grande and is just the place to relax — preferably on the patio — and enjoy a good meal with a glass or two of wine. The interior is decorated with ship's artefacts relating to losses at sea. Reasonably-priced tourist menu.

CASA DA GALÉ
Praia Grande (219 291 218
daily except Mon dinner and
Tuesdays in winter €€
Multibanco debit cards only

fish (grilled, boiled or oven-baked) and **seafood**, *both sold by weight* — so always confirm the weight of your selected fish or shellfish before ordering, otherwise it can become surprisingly expensive.

meat dishes include the typical Portuguese **Carne de Porco à Alentejana** (pork and clams done in the regional way; recipe page 88).

RESTAURANTE DA ADRAGA
Praia da Adraga,
Almoçageme (219 280 028
daily €€

specialises primarily in **local fresh fish** either grilled or in other dishes like *caldeirada* (a fish stew); also *percebes* (barnacles), *sapateira* (crab), *lavagante* (lobster) and *lagosta* (crayfish) — all priced by weight

Other restaurants you might try include the small, rustic **Restaurante da Adraga** nestled into the cliffs, with an unrestricted view of the sea, or the **Restaurante Snack-Bar Cabo da Roca**, perched on the cliff top above the Atlantic at the most westerly point in Continental Europe — with the Serra da Sintra as a backdrop.

RESTAURANTE SNACK- BAR CABO DA ROCA
Cabo da Roca
daily €

light snacks: various sandwiches, *tosta mista* (toasted cheese and ham), *prego no pão* (steak roll), *bifana* (pork roll), hamburgers

light meals including omelettes, various salads, grilled prawns, fish and chips, chicken

restaurants

eat

Pork with clams, Alentejo-style (carne de porco à Alentejana)

Cut the pork into bite-sized pieces and put into a ceramic or glass bowl. Using a pestle and mortar, crush the garlic cloves and the salt to make a paste. Rub this paste into the cubes of pork. Cover and leave in the refrigerator for 24 hours, turning the pork cubes occasionally.

Pork with clams Alentejo-style, as served at the Casa da Galé

In the meantime wash and scrub the cockles well. It is a good idea to leave them soaking in salted water for at least 2 hours. Discard any that have opened.

After the pork has marinated, fry the cubes in the hot fat and, when the pork is almost cooked, add the cockles and the wine. Cover and cook for a further 6-8 minutes, or until the cockles have opened their shells. Discard any that haven't opened.

Sprinkle with the chopped coriander to serve. Traditionally this dish is served with boiled potatoes but chips and salad are just as good. (In the photograph, the dish has been served with home-made crinkled chips.)

Ingredients (for 4 people)

800 g loin of pork
4 garlic cloves
100 g *massa de pimentão**
150 g lard
1 kg cockles
200 ml dry white wine
2 tbsp chopped coriander
salt

**massa de pimentão* (red pepper paste) is available in most Portuguese supermarkets. If unavailable, crush 1 garlic clove with a tsp of salt using a pestle and mortar, add 1 tbsp of sweet paprika and 1 tbsp of oil, mixing well.

recipes

eat

The sandy, often barren countryside south of Lisbon is abruptly broken by the limestone hills on the southern side of the Arrábida Peninsula, giving rise to some quite dramatic coastal scenery between Setúbal and Cabo Espichel in the west. The area has now been designated a Natural Park.

arrábida peninsula

WALK

The objective of the Arrábida Natural Park is to protect the landscape, vegetation and wildlife from the inevitable pressures that exist due to its proximity to Lisbon. There is much to see in this relatively small area and, if you have time to explore, it is well worth visiting the park office in Setúbal; we found the staff there consistently helpful and interested. The walk we describe here is one that the Park Authority established some years ago, although quite a lot of the original waymarking has disappeared. It will give you a pleasant introduction to the inland scenery of Arrábida.

Our timings start at the **Capela São Luís da Serra** (197m). Take the dirt track that leads from the chapel, passing a **wooden signboard** indicating the route. There are red/yellow waymarks here,

Distance: 8.3km/5.1mi; 1h50min (from the Capela São Luís)

Grade: easy-moderate. After a fairly stiff initial ascent of 100m (330ft) most of the walking is easy underfoot and mainly on the level, but there are one or two short, steep sections. *IGE 1:25,000 M888 Series map, sheet 454*

Equipment: see pages 14-15

Transport: from Lisbon take 🚌 561 via Ponte 25 de Abril or 🚌 562 via Ponte Vasco da Gama to Setúbal bus station (Transportes Sul do Tejo, www.tsuldotejo.pt). Either service takes about 1h. Change to 🚌 230 (Sesimbra bus) and ask to alight at the Capela São Luís (journey time 10min). Weekday morning departures at 09.30, 11.45, 13.50. Afternoon returns depart from Sesimbra at 6.15, 17.20, 18.50 and pass by São Luís about 35min after leaving Sesimbra. Travelling by bus, you will need to add 1.4km (25min) to the overall distance and times shown above. Or by 🚗 to/from the Capela São Luís. *Our timings are from the capela and back.*

Refreshments: Bars, cafés and restaurants in nearby Setúbal, none en route

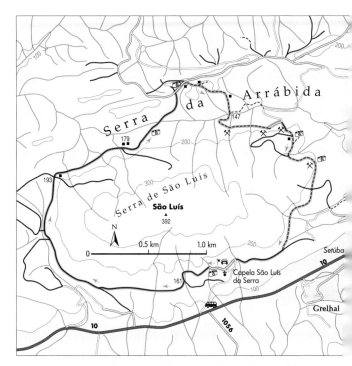

(but these peter out for most of the second half of the walk). The track is initially level, passing through fine umbrella pines, with views down to the coast and Tróia beyond. Then the track starts dropping quite steeply (**4min**) until reaching a T-junction at 161m altitude (**12min**). Turn right here, passing clumps of kermes oak *(Quercus coccifera)* and mastic trees *(Pistacia lentiscus)*. The track narrows to a trail (**15min**) running through a mix of pine and olive trees. When you drop down to join a dirt road coming in from behind and below on the left (**21min**), follow it to the right.

Pass a large **water tank** on the left by an entrance with **green gates** (**30min**) and keep on ahead on the dirt road as it climbs gently, ignoring another dirt road off to the left after just a minute. The road climbs steadily up into more open, cultivated countryside until you reach the **top of the rise** (193m; **36min**) at a crossroads with an old **concrete building** on the right. Keep straight on here, noting the waymark on a pine tree just ahead. You start descending immediately, passing a house called **Casa da Pedreira** on the left, after which the road starts to rise gently again. This rise takes you up to some **old farm buildings** on the left (179m; **47min**).

There are soon views out ahead to the great expanse of flat country beyond the Sado Estuary (visited on Walk 8). The dirt road drops down slightly through olive groves before rising up again and meeting a tarred road (**55min**), where you turn right. Now you have some fine views over to the next ridge to the north, the Serra do Louro, where you'll spot some old windmills.

After following the tarred road for about 100m, you reach an **old ruin** on the right (**57min**); turn right off the road here, on a fairly rough path which initially runs parallel to and below the tarred road. You pass in front of **another ruin** (**59min**), this one on the left. *Take care* at this point, as the path becomes quite indistinct for about 50m. In front of this ruin there is a fork in the path: take the right-hand fork, descending into a shallow

View at the start of the walk near the Capela São Luís da Serra

valley. Soon the path becomes well established (**1h**) and drops down and round to the right of another **ruined building** (**1h04min**). The path is now a dirt trail and drops even further, to a small **concrete bridge** over the watercourse in the bottom of the valley (147m; **1h07min**).

Cross the bridge and follow the trail up to the right. Almost immediately, the trail turns back on itself in a hairpin bend, gains height and then levels off in an **old quarry** (**1h10min**). Pleasant views open out to the hills opposite. Follow the trail through the quarry and on up to the **next abandoned quarry** (**1h14min**), now with the views out over the Sado Estuary beginning to open out. *Take care* here to follow the old road downhill and out of the quarry; initially the surface is dirt, but becomes broken-up tar after just 20 metres.

As the road descends, prepare to leave it at the first sharp bend (where the tarred surface swings back left and continues down to an old barrier): follow a dirt track straight ahead through a **third old quarry**, passing an old **concrete structure with a waymark** (**1h19min**). Continue round the hillside, with

ever more extensive views out
across Setúbal opening up.
The trail narrows to a path at
the far end of the quarry
working (ignore the path
down to the left here).

This path now wends a
delightful way around the
hillside through a mix of
Mediterranean oak, olive,
eucalyptus and thyme until
you emerge in a **fourth small
quarry** (**1h30min**). A short
way further on you cross a
major dirt road and continue
along a trail which narrows to
a path within 50 metres. As
this path contours round the
hillside, you might want to
take home some leaves from the wild rosemary bushes growing
here in profusion.

Entrance to the Castelo São Felipe
in Setúbal

Soon (**1h40min**) you will see some beehives just to the left;
immediately afterwards, you join a dirt trail coming in from the
left. Keep ahead; shortly the red roof and white walls of the
chapel come into view. The fence you have been following on
the left ends at a junction of several tracks; keep ahead on the
main track which immediately joins the dirt road (**1h47min**),
where you turn up right to the **São Luís Chapel** (**1h50min**).

Restaurante Bombordo

Bombordo is a small establishment facing onto the main avenue (Avenida Luisa Todi) behind the waterfront, near the old centre of Setúbal. The restaurant, which spills out onto the pavement, serves only fish, which is cooked on a huge pavement barbecue. Each type of freshly-caught fish is grilled separately and served in recurring sequence — the *rodizio de peixe*. Buskers entertain the customers eating outside under the shade of plane trees.

RESTAURANTE BOMBORDO
Avenida Luisa Todi, 536, Setúbal
(**(mobile) 917 306 705**
daily, except Mondays €

the **speciality** is *rodizio de peixe*: *sardinhas* (sardines), *rodovalho* (halibut), *salmão* (salmon), *peixe espada* (swordfish), *cherne* (turbot), *chocos* (squid), *salmonetes* (red mullet) or whatever is in season — it just keeps coming and coming.

Served with potatoes boiled in their skins and a fresh green salad. *Azeitonas* (olives), country-style bread, and a carafe of local wine accompany this marathon.

To finish choose from fruit (in season) or *doce de laranja* (orange roll; recipe opposite) — with a glass of the local Moscatel (a sweet fortified wine from Setúbal).

Rodizio de peixe and (opposite) orange roll, as served at Bombordo

restaurants

eat

Rodizio de peixe

Why not try your own? For 4 people buy approximately 2.5 kg of a variety of fish such as those listed on the Bombordo menu — or any that you would like to try. The fishmonger will clean them for you if you ask, but sardines are normally left whole for grilling.

Wash the fish in cold water and dry. Sprinkle with sea salt and leave covered in the refrigerator for a few hours. When grilling, make sure the grill is hot (the coals should be white) before adding the fish. Grill each type of fish independently and serve, then grill the next type and so on.

Serve with jacket potatoes, a fresh green salad, plenty of slices of lemon, and local wine.

Orange roll *(doce de laranja or torta de laranja de Setúbal)*

Whisk the eggs and sugar together. Dissolve the cornflour in the orange juice and add the grated orange rind. Add the mixture to the eggs and sugar; mix well.

Grease a Swiss-roll baking tray (20.5 x 30.5 cm) with butter and line the tray with baking paper. Grease the lining paper and sprinkle with sugar. Pour the mixture into the baking tray and bake (160°C) for about 25min, until firm and golden.

Turn out onto a tea towel well sprinkled with sugar. Trim off any crisp edges and carefully roll up with the help of the tea towel. When cold, place on a serving dish and sprinkle with sugar. The roll will create its own sauce when left for a while.

Ingredients (for 4-6 people)
150 ml pure orange juice
5 large eggs
1 rounded tbsp cornflour
200 g caster sugar
grated rind of 1 orange

recipes

eat

This walk takes you into the heart of a rice-producing area. The terrain is flat and may seem uninteresting initially, but you will encounter a wealth of flowers and bird life. Above all you will experience a unique feeling of isolation — strangely accentuated by the proximity of Setúbal's heavy industry on the far side of the estuary.

sado's rice paddies

WALK

During the winter months the rice fields by the Sado Estuary lie fallow, and since this period coincides with the major bird migrations, this can often be the best time to see the bird life — which on this walk is exceptional.

Indeed, it could be argued that after half an hour of walking through rice fields you will have had enough, but even a walker with only a modest interest in ornithology cannot fail to be impressed with the fauna on display. Depending on the time of year you are likely to see grey heron *(Ardea cinerea),* purple heron *(Ardea purpurea),* white storks *(Ciconia ciconia),* little egrets *(Egretta garzetta),* avocets *(Recurvirostra avosetta),* marsh harriers *(Circus aeruginosus),* black kites *(Milvus migrans)* and many others. So … plenty to keep you going a little further!

Distance: 15.8km/9.8mi; 3h05min (a linear walk, which can be shortened by returning at any point)

Grade: easy, level walking, but there is *no shade. IGE 1:25,000 M888 Series map, sheets 466, 475*

Equipment: see pages 14-15; take *plenty of water,* sunhats and clothing to protect from sun- and wind-burn.

Transport: 🚌 from Lisbon to Setúbal as on page 85. Or 🚌 to Setúbal ferry terminal. At Setúbal bus station check bus times from Tróia to Comporta and back (vary according to season and Tróia ferry sailings). From the station, walk through little back streets down to Avenida Luisa Todi (where Restaurante Bombordo, featured on page 90, is located), then follow this left for 500m, to the Tróia ferry terminal (half-hourly service; the crossing takes about 20min). A single ticket costs €1.0 per person; a car plus driver €5.0 (car passengers additional to the driver pay €1.0). Look out for dolphins as you cross! On the far side either take the connecting bus (the bus stop is 50m up the road from the ferry) or a taxi to Comporta. This will take another 20min.

Refreshments:
cafés, bars and restaurants in Setúbal and Comporta; none en route

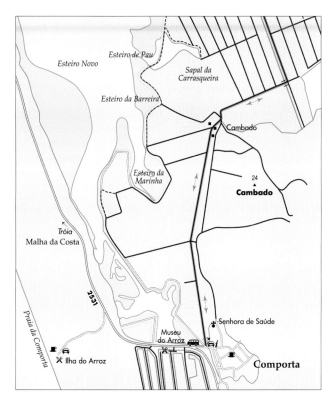

As you come into Comporta, look out for the Restaurante Museu do Arroz (Rice Museum Restaurant) on the right just as you enter the village; this is where you will eat. The bus stop is just beyond it; if you are in a taxi, get the driver to drop you off at the bus stop. Walk along the main road towards the village

Bank in Comporta, with the obligatory stork's nest

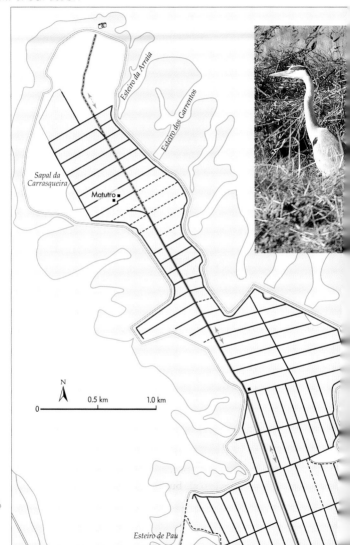

Esteiro da Arraia

Esteiro dos Garrentos

Sapal da
Carrasqueira

Matutro

N

0   0.5 km   1.0 km

Esteiro de Pau

Opposite: grey heron; above: typical barn made with reeds and planking, near Comporta

and, 50m beyond the restaurant, turn down left off the main road and walk between the old blue and white town gateposts. Just after these, turn left on a dirt road, passing a notice board for the Sado Estuary Natural Park and a blue 'P' sign (if you have come by car, park here). *Walk timings are from this point.*

Start out at the **natural park notice board:** walk along the dirt road immediately ahead of you, keeping the tall **cane hedges** on your right. You immediately see the first **rice fields** off to the left and will start to pass small sheds containing pumps for irrigating the rice. At a fork (**9min**) keep straight ahead, still on a dirt road, but now less used and with grass down the centre. At a crossroads (**14min**), keep straight on — noticing (depending on the time of year) the small vegetable patches on the right, often with seaweed compost spread over the sandy soil.

Before long you come to a small group of houses and sheds (**Cambado; 21min**). Keep straight on between them and, at the far end, turn left at the T-junction (there may be some noisy dogs on your left, but they should all be chained up). Immediately afterwards, where the dirt road divides, bear right and keep straight on until you cross the **main irrigation channel** (**30min**). Immediately after crossing this, turn left on a well-used dirt road which runs parallel to the irrigation channel.

Eventually you reach a junction, with an **iron grid** and **small concrete building** on the right and a **concrete valve housing** on the left (**48min**). Over to the left, 10m away, is a **water channel**. It is worth taking a look here for waders, including avocets. There are various tracks leading off from the opposite side of the main dirt road, and following these can be quite rewarding for bird-spotters.

Turn right on the road and when the road swings off left (**1h12min**), walk straight ahead on a lesser track (you may need to negotiate an electric fence). You pass some old buildings off to the left at **Matutro** and, continuing ahead, you come to a **gate** (**1h38min**). Just beyond is the Sado River estuary, with views over to Setúbal and its heavy industry.

From here retrace your steps, keeping on the main dirt road when you reach it once more, to return to the **natural park noticeboard** (**3h05min**).

While rice features extensively in Portuguese cooking, you may not realise that Portugal is quite a significant producer; in 1995 the country produced 124,500 tonnes, rising in 2003 to 146,000 tonnes.

The average per capita annual consumption of rice in Portugal is 16 kg; this is the highest level in the European Union and totals some 300,000 tonnes per annum. About half the rice consumed is grown within Portugal, and about 45% of that production comes from the Alentejo (the rest from Ribatejo, Beira Litoral and Estremadura).

The flat rice paddies are ploughed using cage-wheeled tractors and then irrigated ready for sowing in May. About three weeks later the water is drained to encourage root development. Irrigation then continues until one or two weeks ahead of harvest (late October, when the water is drained off). Normally about 6 tonnes of rice are produced per hectare.

The huge expanse of rice fields near Comporta is a haven for bird life, especially in winter, when the fields lie fallow and birds are migrating.

Museu do Arroz

This restaurant is situated in the old rice warehouse and drying plant. Pictures of the old rice factory decorate the walls, together

with some quite bizarre decor including flying herons. It is just like eating in a museum and, as you might imagine, rice is a very prominent ingredient on the menu. *Petiscos* (little tastes) cover the table: tasty rice balls, fresh and mature sheeps' cheeses, quails' eggs with a lovely 'rose' sauce, country bread and olives. Don't forget that the *petiscos* will be added to your bill! For the adventurous we have chosen their razor-shell and cockle rice recipe (see page 102).

If you prefer a restaurant on the beach. try the **Ilha do Arroz** which is under the same ownership

restaurants

eat

MUSEU DO ARROZ
Comporta
(265 497 555/fax 265 497 600
daily except Monday, lunch and dinner €€
Multibanco debit cards only

good selection of **petiscos** (little snacks); see photograph opposite

rice dishes are obviously the **speciality**, but there are also varied **salads**, **grilled fish** or **steaks**, with a selection of **sweets** to follow.

the *vinho de casa* (**house wine**) is a very acceptable red from Cartuxo

Beach by the Restaurante Ilha do Arroz; left: rice ball and (opposite): *petiscos*, both at the Museu do Arroz

ILHA DO ARROZ
Praia da Comporta
(265 490 510/fax 265 490 511
daily except Wednesday, lunch and dinner €€
Multibanco debit cards only

good choice of **salads, soup** and **petiscos** (little snacks) — including *gambas à guilho* (prawns in garlic), *ovos mexidos com farinheira* (scrambled eggs with sausages), and *amêijoas à Bulhão Pato* (cockles Bulhão Pato-style; recipe page 105).

rice also features here, with *arroz de tamboril* (monkfish rice), *arroz de polvo* (octopus rice), *arroz do mar* (seafood rice) and *arroz de pato* (duck rice; recipe on page 104)

steaks and **fried fish**, both served with tomato rice

as the Museu do Arroz and situated on the beach at Comporta, about 200 yards from the main road. This restaurant/bar is just the place to while away an afternoon, especially after enjoying a snack or lunch washed down with a jug of *sangria*).

WAYS WITH RICE — MUSEU DO ARROZ

Razor-shell and cockle rice (arroz de langueirão)

Clean the *langueirões* and cockles in salted water to remove any particles of sand. When cleaned put the *langueirões* and cockles in a saucepan of salted water over a high heat until they open.

Remove the *langueirões* from their shells, but leave the cockles in their shells (after discarding any that haven't opened). Put the cockles to one side and reserve the water.

Chop the onion, pepper and garlic and fry in the olive oil. When the onion is opaque, add the chopped coriander or parsley and the reserved water. The water will need to be about 3 times the volume of the rice; add more water if necessary. Add the washed rice and *langueirões*.

Cook gently until the rice is soft — the mixture should not be too dry. Just before serving add the cooked cockles and stir together.

Ingredients (for 4 people)

12 *langueirões* (razor-shell clams)
24 cockles
300 g rice (the restaurant uses local 'arroz carolino', which can be bought at the nearby Atlantic Rice Company)
4 tbsp olive oil
1 large onion
1 green or red pepper or a mixture of both
1 garlic clove
coriander or parsley, chopped
salt

Sweet rice pudding (*arroz doce*)

Wash the rice, then add to a saucepan of salted boiling water. Bring to the boil and cook the rice for 2 minutes. In another saucepan boil the milk with the lemon peel and cinnamon stick.

Drain the rice and rinse under cold water. Add to the boiling milk, bring milk to the boil again, stir and leave to cook, uncovered, on a low heat for about 30 minutes, or until the milk has been absorbed and the rice is soft.

Remove from the heat, take out the pieces of lemon rind and cinnamon stick. Then quickly stir in the sugar, beaten egg yolks and butter. Return the rice to a very low heat and cook slowly for a few minutes, *without boiling*, to cook the egg yolks.

Pour the mixture into individual shallow dishes or one large shallow dish, to a thickness of about 2 cm. Decorate with cinnamon and chill for 1-2 hours.

Ingredients (for 4 people)
125 g short-grain rice
120 g caster sugar
750 ml milk
3 egg yolks
40 g butter
1 tsp salt
3-4 strips of lemon peel
1 cinnamon stick and ground
  cinnamon

recipes

eat

WAYS WITH RICE — ILHA DO ARROZ

Duck rice (*arroz de pato*)

Cook the duck, remove the skin and shred the flesh. Reserve the cooking water. Cook the rice in plenty of boiling salted water.

When the rice is cooked, strain and pour boiling water over it, then drain. Add the shredded pieces of duck, the currants and the pine nuts. If the mixture is too dry, add some of the reserved cooking water.

Season with salt and a dash of *piri-piri*. Put the mixture into a shallow oven-proof dish, garnish with the slices of *chouriço* and cook in a moderate oven for 15-20 minutes.

Left and opposite: the recipes as served at Ilha do Arroz. Previous pages: razor-shell and cockle rice at the Museu do Arroz and sweet rice pudding made at home

<u>Ingredients (for 4 people)</u>
1 duck (2.5 kg)
300 g long-grain rice
1 *chouriço* sausage (spicy sausage)
40 g pine nuts
40 g currants
salt
piri-piri (see page 142)

recipes

eat

Cockles Bulhão Pato-style
(amêijoas à Bulhão Pato)

This dish originates from Lisbon and is associated with the Portuguese Romantic poet, Raimundo Bulhão Pato (1837-1912), who had creative gastronomic skills. Although he lived mostly just south of Lisbon, he spent time in Sintra and Colares with other well-known literary figures of the day.

Wash and scrub clean the cockles in salted water, changing the water several times (or leave them to soak for 2 hours before using).

Heat the olive oil and fry the chopped garlic cloves until they are beginning to colour. Add the cockles and the finely chopped coriander and season with salt and pepper.

Fry gently, shaking the pan occasionally, until the cockles have opened. Discard any that have not opened. Sprinkle with lemon juice and serve with slices of lemon.

Ingredients (for 4 people)
1 kg cockles (amêijoas)
2 tbsp olive oil
2 garlic cloves
1 lemon
1 bunch of coriander
salt and pepper

Mafra is dominated by a huge convent-palace dating from the early 18th century. This walk approaches the town from an angle that allows you to appreciate its scale. On the way you pass one of Wellington's hill fortifications, part of his system of defences against the French in the Peninsula Wars of 1810.

mafra

WALK

Start the walk at **Ericeira bus station**. Turn left and walk along to the intersection with the main Mafra/Sintra road. Turn right downhill here and, just 20m below the junction, look for the 'Superbock' sign on the other side of the main road. Turn in by this sign, initially on tarmac. When the tarmac runs out (**5min**) keep on ahead on a dirt track, passing the **Quinta das Meninas** on the right (**6min**). In under another minute you will reach another house, where the dirt road ends.

Just beyond the second gate to this house you will find a narrow footpath: follow this up the side of the valley, keeping to the right-hand side

Distance: 11.9km/7.4mi; 2h32min

Grade: easy. Mostly level walking and easy underfoot. Care is needed on the final stretch along the road into the centre of Mafra. *IGE 1:25,000 M888 Series map, sheets 388, 402*

Equipment: see pages 14-15

Transport: 🚌 Mafrense bus service from Campo Grande in Lisbon to Ericeira, same bus to return from Mafra. Journey time to Ericeira about 1h10min; return from Mafra to Lisbon (40km) about 55min. Up-to-date times can be found at www.rodest.pt

Refreshments en route: Ericeira at the start of the walk, cafés at Lapa da Serra and Zambujal, Mafra at the end of the walk

Opening times/prices:
Mafra Palace daily from 09.30-18.00 ex Tue/holidays; €3.00
Tapada (zoological gardens) daily from 10.00-16.00; book ahead by telephoning (261 817 050

of the field reached a minute later. You pass a **ruined building** on the left (**12min**) and a minute later rise up onto tarmac again, in a new **housing development**. Turn left on the tarmac; you can already see Mafra, the end of the walk, in the far distance! Take the first right turn, then a left turn (all on tarmac), then fork right downhill on a concrete walkway with lamp posts.

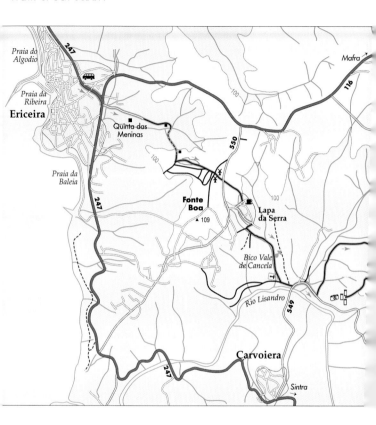

This will bring you to a tarmac T-junction (**16min**), where you first turn left, then immediately right onto a footpath. Follow the path to a small tarmac road and keep ahead, slightly uphill. At a fork, turn right, initially on a pavement. You join another tarmac road which takes you to a **pair of windmills** by an open tarmac area called **Praçete Figueira** (**20min**). Turn left beside the second windmill (which has been restored) and follow a dirt track. This forks almost immediately: bear left, descending in front of a long-abandoned half-finished **concrete structure**. Just beyond this you will see a **red brick wall**. Take the path alongside this wall, down to the road below (**22min**) and cross the road to enter **Lapa da Serra**.

Pass to the right of **Café Retiro de Caçador** (**24min**) and continue along the main street through the village until it begins to drop downhill. At this point, turn sharp right on Rua do Poço (also signposted to 'n. Senhora da Ó'; **26min**), to

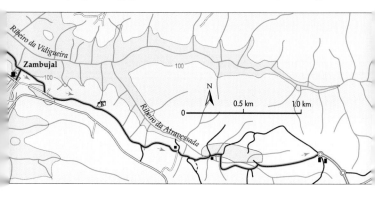

continue dropping sharply downhill, away from the village. After two minutes of zigzagging down on tarmac, fork left on the narrower lane (also signposted to 'n. Senhora da Ó'; **28min**). Wind down this country lane, passing the fountain **Bico Vale de**

View down to the market gardens in the Ribeira da Vidigueira

Cancela on the left (**30min**) and emerging by the **cemetery** (**33min**). In another minute you join the main road by a small bridge; do *not* cross the bridge, but turn left and walk along the road. Ignore the first dirt road off left half a minute later; continue ahead. Then, just as the main road begins to rise from the valley floor, turn left on another dirt road (**36min**). This skirts around the foot of the **Serra do Forte** and then begins to rise slightly, just above the valley of the **Ribeira da Vidigueira** (**42min**). The valley floor is intensively cultivated, with vegetable and fruit farming providing a constant source of interest as you look down on the fields. Ignore the turning off left (**48min**) and continue ahead on the now steadily-rising track. Eventually this main dirt track swings sharply up to the right, and a lesser, grassy track goes straight ahead (**57min**). The route to Mafra is straight ahead, but first its worth exploring the old hill fortifications dating from the Peninsula Wars and forming part of Wellington's Lines of Torres Vedras. So turn up right here, into the village of **Zambujal**.

Then walk up the dirt road until you reach a tarmac road. Turn right and follow this road up out of the village for four minutes, until the tarmac ends. From here a dirt road takes you to a flat hilltop, where you will find the **old**

The Lines of Torres Vedras

The Anglo-Portuguese armies under Wellington's command had been forced back from the Spanish border in September 1810, but the French commander, Masséna, did not realise that Wellington had prepared for this eventuality. Twelve months earlier Wellington had surveyed the country to the north of Lisbon and commissioned the building of three lines of defence: the most northerly (Line 1) ran from the river Sizandro to Alhandra on the Tagus; the second from Ribeira de São Lourenço to Póvoa de Santa Iria (also on the Tagus); the third and final line of defence (in case of evacuation) at São Julião da Barra, west of Lisbon.

Work on the fortifications started in November 1809 and within a year 130 of the 152 forts had been completed. By the end of October 1810 there were almost 40,000 troops manning the lines. Masséna had no idea of their existence; he was a long way from home, and winter was setting in. After relatively limited skirmishes he retreated.

Perhaps the most impressive fort is that at São Vicente, just outside Torres Vedras, which can be visited. The Torres Vedras Museum has an excellent display and models of The Lines.

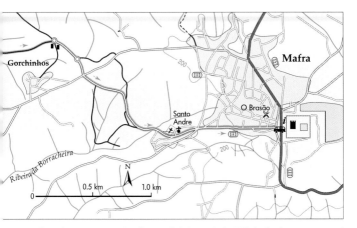

fortifications at the far end (**1h09min**). While little remains of the fortifications themselves, it is easy to see the general layout and deep trench surrounding the fort. The vantage point is remarkable, and one can imagine the purpose of this particular installation being to guard the road below.

For a detailed description of Wellington's Lines of Torres Vedras, the British Historical Society has published a book on the subject: *The Lines of Torres Vedras*, by A H Norris and R W Bremner (details at www.bhsportugal.org).

After visiting the fort, retrace your steps to the junction at the 57min-point of your outgoing route. Now walk on along the grassy track, passing a **white building** on your right (**1h21min**). In two minutes you will rise up onto tarmac, where you will see a narrow footpath off to the left. Follow this path down to a **washhouse** reached half a minute later. From here follow the tarmac lane ahead uphill for half a minute, to a T-junction with a tarmac road, where you turn left (Rua da Feiteira). This road soon becomes a dirt track (**1h28min**).

The track rises gently between vineyards and high cane windbreaks to the crest of a small rise (**1h31min**), from where you can see the imposing palace of Mafra ahead in the distance — now sadly surrounded by an unfortunate

Cornus sanguinea

urban sprawl. The track now becomes a sandy trail, where you might look out for clumps of the plant shown above, *Cornus sanguinea,* on the left. You pass a concrete structure on the right, followed by a **park area** behind high wire fencing, also on the right. When the trail divides (by an old stone wall up to the right; **1h38min**), ignore the grassy track leading off to the right. Keep straight ahead on the trail.

You emerge by a small house, where a tarmac lane comes in from above and to the right (**1h42min**). Ignore this lane; walk past the house and follow a descending dirt track which then rises to meet a wider dirt road (**1h44min**), which you follow straight ahead. The road takes you down to a stream (**Ribeiro da Atravessada**; **1h46min**), which is crossed on a culvert. Walk

Mafra Palace was created as the result of a vow made by Dom João V who ruled Portugal from 1706 to 1750. This was in many ways Portugal's golden era.

But Dom João was still childless after three years of marriage, so he vowed to build a monastery should God give him an heir. Following the birth of a daughter, he fulfilled his vow in grandiose style with the building of Mafra Palace.

The building is made principally of limestone and marble, this giving the exterior a wonderfully warm aspect. It is said that up to 50,000 workers were involved in the construction, which took place between 1717 and 1735. The main, west-facing façade is no less than 220 metres long. The building itself occupies some 40,000 square metres, and the two towers attain 68 metres and house over 100 bells.

Adjoining the palace is the 'Tapada', a park enclosed by a 25km-long wall, with a zoological garden open to the public.

up the far side towards an **old ruin**, now on a new dirt road which leads up towards new housing. Zigzag up above the ruin, coming almost immediately to a T-junction in the **new development**. Turn right here, now on the level. Where this dirt road swings up left (**1h49min**), take an old cart track leading off to the right, descending once again to the valley floor (**1h52min**).

Ahead of you, just on the other side of the valley, is a dirt track leading straight up out of the valley. Instead of following this, *turn left* up a lesser dirt track which rises alongside the valley floor. Bear left at the T-junction (**1h54min**), still on a dirt track and still continuing up alongside the shallow valley. Just before a small field (a dead end), the track swings up to the left through a small hedge (**1h57min**). By now the track has dwindled to a trail; it rises to a dirt road (**1h58min**), where you turn right towards some blocks of flats. Past the flats, you emerge on tarmac at a roundabout on the outskirts of **Mafra** (**2h02min**).

Turn right here and walk along this road to the next roundabout, reached three minutes later. Keep straight on here for half a minute, to a main road. Cross over and follow the wide road on the far side. This winds down past the **cemetery** on your left (**2h13min**) and then swings round past the **Igreja Santo Andre**, also on your left (**2h15min**). From here bear right downhill past **Quinta Corredoura** on your right. The road ahead leads straight up to magnificent **Mafra Palace** (**2h32min**); you'll get imposing views and be amazed at the sheer scale of the structure, as it dwarfs the lesser buildings you pass on the way up.

O Brasão

This very popular restaurant is tucked away from the main tourist areas around Mafra Palace. If you want to try authentic traditional Portuguese food, this restaurant is a *must*. The locals throng here, especially on Sundays.

Restaurante O Brasão

RESTAURANTE O BRASÃO
Travessa Manuel Esteves, 7
Mafra (261 815 687
daily €
Multibanco debit cards only

specialities include *cozida a Portuguesa* (beef, chicken, pork, etc all boiled together to make a stew), *ensopada de enguias* (eel stew) and *lombo de porco recheada com alheira* (loin of pork stuffed with a special sausage; see recipe opposite).

Apart from the specialities shown above (and there are more besides), there is a wide range of grilled fresh fish and meat.

If you still have room left you will be offered the usual range of sweets, including a huge chunk of *pudim* (a dense crème caramel).

restaurants

eat

Loin of pork stuffed with a flour-and-pork sausage, seasoned with garlic and paprika
(lombo de porco recheada com alheira)

Open out the loin of pork, making an incision lengthwise. Season with salt and pepper, and spread the crushed garlic on the cut surface.

Place the sausage* along the length of the roast, without removing the skin, and then close the halves and tie together with string.

Put in a roasting tin and baste with olive oil. Roast fat side up for about an hour at 175°C. Leave to rest for 15-20 minutes before slicing.

Serve with Arabian-style rice (rice with chopped nuts and currants), chips and salad. Note that in Portugal it is not at all unusual to serve both rice and potatoes in one meal!

*To make your own *alheira* (gluten-free if you wish), use 6 parts sausage meat to 2 parts breadcrumbs, paprika and garlic to taste. There are plenty of sources for sausage casings on the web, where you can also find the interesting history of the *alheira* and the full recipe in English.

Ingredients (for 4 people)
1.2 kg loin of pork
1 *alheira* sausage (a sausage made with pork and wheat flour, seasoned with garlic and paprika)
2 garlic cloves
1 tbsp olive oil
salt and pepper

recipes
eat

Lourinhã's fame is due largely to the significant palae-
ontological finds in the Jurassic limestones that outcrop
along the nearby coastal cliffs. Palaeontology and the
Jurassic conjure up visions of dinosaurs, and almost
everywhere in the town you will see references to the
fossil remains found locally.

lourinhã's dinosaurs

WALK

Lourinhã lies some 65km north of Lisbon, just inland from the coast. The town itself is pleasant and has the atmosphere of a bustling centre for the local agricultural industry. This walk takes you from Lourinhã town centre (after a visit to the excellent dinosaur exhibits in the museum) out to the coast and then northwards past the fine sands of Praia Areia Branca to the coastal fort of Pai Mogo, where fossil dinosaur eggs have been found.

The bus station is quite close to the old town centre of **Lourinhã**. First walk to the museum: turn right as you come out of the bus station and, at the roundabout, take the second left exit (Rua Miguel Bombarda). Soon you come into a small square (Praça Marquês de Pombal); leave this by following Rua 5 de Outubro. At a T-junction which comes up immediately, turn right. Now the **Lourinhã Museum** is just on your left.

The museum has various sections, including a good display focussing on traditional agriculture. There is also an excep-

Distance: 7.7km/4.8mi; 1h54min (one way)

Grade: easy-moderate. Generally on good paths, and mostly waymarked. There are one or two steep gradients, but these are fairly short in duration. *IGE 1:25,000 M888 Series map, sheet 349*

Equipment: see pages 14-15

Transport: 🚌 Rede Expresso bus from Lisbon to Lourinhã and return; journey time about 1h20min. Departures from Lisbon at 07.00, 08.00 (not Sun), 09.00 (Mon-Fri), 10.00, 11.45, 12.15; departures from Lourinhã at 14.55, 16.25, 17.25, 18.55. Up-to-date information at www.rede-expressos.pt

Refreshments en route: cafés, restaurants in Lourinhã (start of the walk), Praia da Areia Branca (see page 126); café/restaurant at Forte de Parmaigo (end of the walk)

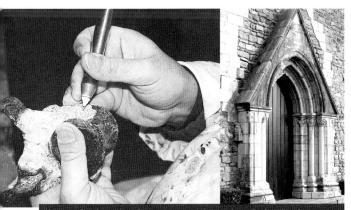

Cleaning fossils in Lourinhã's museum and Lourinhã's Gothic church

tionally well displayed and documented exhibition of dinosaur fossils, many collected locally from the route of this walk. You can either visit the museum now or when you return to Lourinhã; either way, it's not to be missed!

Our walk proper starts from the front of the **museum** (18m). With your back to the entrance, turn left and take the second left turn, by the Café Central, along Rua da Misericordia. There is a sign here to 'Igreja do Castelo' and also a sign for the waymarked walk to Forte de Pai Mogo. Walk round to the left of the 16th-century church, the **Igreja do Castelo** (**2min**), noting its simple Gothic line. Then continue down the tarmac lane from the main entrance of the church, passing the **cemetery** off to your left. You come to a signpost for the PR1 footpath, 'Labrusque 2.3km' (**5min**). Turn left downhill here, now on a

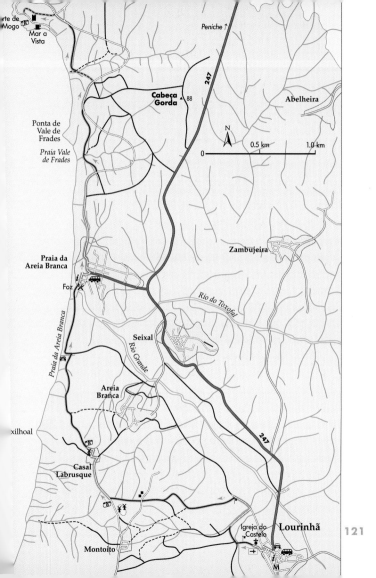

rte de
Mogo

Mar a
Vista

Peniche ↑

247

Cabeça
Gorda

88

Abelheira

Ponta de
Vale de
Frades

*Praia Vale
de Frades*

N

0   0.5 km   1.0 km

Zambujeira

Praia da
Areia Branca

Foz

Praia da Areia Branca

Rio do Toxofal

Seixal

Rio Grande

Areia
Branca

xilhoal

Casal
Labrusque

247

Montoito

Igreja do
Castelo

Lourinhã

M

gravel road which crosses a smelly stream a minute later.

Just over the stream you emerge on a major dirt road, where you turn right. At a T-junction with a tarmac road (**7min**), turn right again, and follow this road to another T-junction (**10min**). Turn left, following the road until you come to another PR1 signpost, then turn left off the tarmac onto a dirt road (**12min**). This track starts rising gently as you pass through an area of orchards sheltered with high cane windbreaks (**14min**). Three minutes later the track swings right and levels off, then starts climbing again. On reaching a tarmac road (**31min**), cross over and join a dirt road on the far side, passing some houses on the right. The road rises past some old **windmills** off to the left.

At the top of the hill (90m; **35min**) the dirt road levels off, and in another two minutes you come out to a T-junction with a tarmac road and sea views ahead. In the spring the fields here are bordered by swathes of yellow *Oxalis pes-caprea* which, although very pretty, is regarded by the farmers as a problem weed. Turn right at the T-junction, and the road will lead you into the hamlet of **Casal Labrusque**.

Continue on the main road through the houses until the road starts to descend (**44min**), at which point you turn left (just before a sign wishing you 'Boa viagem'). In another half minute, turn right by an **old windmill**, and then turn left just beyond this same windmill into Rua do Moinho. Now you have some fine views down to Praia Areia Branca.

The tarmac ends and a dirt track comes under foot (**46min**); follow the track as it swings to the right, between high cane windbreaks. Look out for the tiny, delicate purple flowers of

Walking through the orchards north of Lourinhã

Fumaria officinalis which can be found along the wayside in this area. The dirt track becomes sandy and reduces to a trail (**53min**), as you drop down towards the beach.

When you come to a major dirt road (**59min**), left leads to the beach car park and right (the waymarked route) to Seixal. (Note at this point that the waymarking for the PR1 will lead you round through Seixal to Praia de Areia Branca, a detour of nearly 2.5km and nearly all on tarmac. The reason for this is the need to cross the Rio Grande as it flows out onto the beach just before Praia da Areia Branca village. In fact, this can almost always be crossed on the beach, unless there has been exceptionally heavy winter rain or there is a very high tide. We therefore suggest you try this direct route which is shorter and far more pleasant.)

So turn left onto the beach, **Praia da Areia Branca** and, heading north, cross the stream to find yourself just below Foz, a bar-café/restaurant (**1h09min**). If you continue along the beach you will find steps up onto the small promenade just a couple of minutes beyond the restaurant (our lunch suggestion; see overleaf).

Continue north along the promenade until you are led up to the right of the youth hostel (**Pousada de Juventude**; **1h15min**). Turn left after the hostel, walking up the road (waymarked) and turning left again out of the new **housing developments of Praia da Areia Branca**. Still on the road, you reach the top of the rise (**1h22min**), and the road starts to descend. Three minutes downhill, watch for a turn-off left *(not waymarked):* take this dirt road (**1h25min**), which leads to the next beach, the **Praia Vale de Frades** (**1h27min**).

Climb up the far side on the dirt track, to come out on the next headland (**Ponta de Vale de Frades**), where you will find a narrow dirt trail above the tarmac road (**1h32min**). Continue on this, parallel with the road at first, but after half a minute heading left, climbing towards the headland. At an area with cane windbreaks, where the road is just off to the right

(**1h35min**), walk back to the road (waymarked) and turn left. In just over a minute you pass a vehicle lay-by. Turn left off the road (**1h40min**), following waymarks down a small footpath which leads towards the next beach. Take care, a minute after leaving the road, to turn *right* by a waymark (which doesn't indicate which way to go!). *Be careful too, if the ground is wet;* the marly soil here can be slippery.

You descend to a small stream at the bottom of the valley by a metal-roofed shed, just above the next, unnamed beach (**1h44min**). You now join a wide dirt track which takes you up onto the next headland (**1h48min**). At the top you rejoin the tarmac road and turn left. Follow the road until you can take a footpath off left to **Forte de Pai Mogo** (44m; **1h54min**). The fort dates from 1674 and was one of a line of coastal defences set up between Peniche to the north down to the Tagus in the south. It was also intended to protect the easy landing offered by the beach at Areia Branca from seaborne invaders. The fort has remained largely unaltered since it was built, but is due to be extensively restored in the near future. The headland on which it stands is also of considerable geological interest, being the site where the dinosaur eggs displayed in Lourinhã Museum were discovered. Dinosaur footprints have also been found in the vicinity.

At the bottom of the road there is a small café/restaurant, Mar a Vista, where you can have some refreshments and telephone for a Lourinhã taxi to fetch you (℃ 261 413 280 or 261 459 117). Alternatively, retrace your steps to Lourinhã — a total walking time of 3h48min.

Foz

This bar-café and restaurant's appeal is not only in the food, but the incredible feeling of being a part of the sea, sand and sky as you enjoy your meal perched on the end of a rocky outcrop right on the beach.

The menu offers a wide range of dishes, from light meals and snacks to hearty Portuguese fare.

Caldeirada de peixe as served at Foz; opposite: assembling the ingredients at home

FOZ
Praia da Areia Branca, Lourinhã
(mobile) ℘ 918 620 994
daily except Thursdays €-€€

Selections from the *regional menu:*

light meals, including omelettes and sandwiches

speciality is locally-caught **fish** and **shellfish** — simply grilled or incorporated into traditional dishes like *caldeirada de peixe* (a fish stew, see recipe opposite)

selection of **grilled meats,** including steak, pork chops and veal cutlets

restaurants

eat

Fish stew
(caldeirada de peixe)

In the bottom of a heavy-based saucepan put the finely sliced onion rings and chopped garlic cloves. On top of this put the sliced potatoes, strips of red pepper and chopped tomatoes (skinned and seeds removed).

Tear the bay leaf and add together with the finely chopped coriander and wine. Season with the olive oil, pepper and sweet paprika. Cover and cook, occasionally shaking the pan, do not stir.

Cut the fish into large pieces and, when the potatoes are nearly cooked, add the fish and shellfish in alternate layers. Season with salt and continue cooking until the fish and shellfish are ready.

Serve from the same saucepan, ensuring everyone has a portion of all the layers. Top with fried bread (optional).

Ingredients (for 4 people)

1.5 kg of mixed fish
500 g prawns (or other types of shellfish)
2 onions, finely sliced
2 cloves of garlic, chopped
1 red pepper, in strips
450 g ripe tomatoes, chopped
500 g potatoes, finely sliced
200 ml white wine
1 tbsp olive oil
1 bay leaf
2 tsp sweet paprika
1 bunch of coriander, finely chopped
salt and pepper
4 slices of fried bread (optional)

recipes

eat

127

Today Alcochete's pleasantly sleepy atmosphere belies its past importance as a favourite hunting ground for kings João I and II. However, its history goes back much further, as it was apparently a centre for the production of domestic ceramics in Roman times, making use of the locally abundant water, wood, clay and sand.

alcochete

EXCURSION

From 17th century the town became an important producer of salt (the old flats are still visible), and a significant local fishing industry also developed. Many of the buildings in the town date from this period. These industries both declined from the mid-20th century, and Alcochete increasingly became a backwater as new communication links to the south bypassed it.

But Alcochete suddenly leapt back into prominence with the building of the new Vasco da Gama bridge, not least because the bridge impinged on the Tagus Estuary Natural Reserve, an internationally recognised bird sanctuary. The bridge won.

Transport: ⚓ from the Estação Fluvial at Terreiro do Paço (south of the Praça do Comércio) to Seixalinho (*not* Seixal); half-hourly departures; crossing takes 20min. Then taxi from the terminal to Alcochete (20min; approx €7.50). For the return there are regular 🚐 buses back to Lisbon (from Avenida 5 de Outubro); journey time 20min to the Estação Oriente at the Parque das Nações (see page 28)

Refreshments: at Alcochete (see page 131)

Opening hours:
Park office, Tagus Estuary Natural Reserve: weekdays 09.30-13.00; 14.00-17.30; ☏ 212 348 021

Area map: see page 134

With the new bridge and improved fluvial links, the town is rapidly becoming a dormitory for Lisbon. To date, this has not spoilt its pleasant mid 50's atmosphere.

Leaving Seixalinho, a new ferry terminal on the south side of the river, ask the taxi driver to drop you at **Alcochete's tourist office (turismo)**, which is quite central. Pick up a map of the town, then just spend some time looking around the narrow streets, with rows of typical fishermen's houses, the simple lines

Bright tiles decorate some houses on a street in Alcochete

of the church and the pretty little central square where, almost certainly, you will find the male population of the town holding their daily 'parliament'.

Do call in at the **Centro Interpretação** for the **Reserva Natural do Estuário do Tejo**. Established in 1976, the reserve covers over 14,000 hectares, has a resident population of flamingoes and attracts huge populations of migratory species, including half the European population of wintering avocets. Happily, some seven years on, the 'marriage' of bridge and bird life does not seem to have been too unfortunate. Ask at the office for information on guided walks in the protected area.

There are plenty of local restaurants to choose from in Alcochete but, if you would like to try something different , we recommend the **Restaurante Solar do Peixe** (closed Monday evening and all day Wednesday), which is opposite 'Turismo' and facing onto the Tagus estuary. This restaurant serves a fish stew called *cataplana de tamboril* (*cataplana* of monkfish).

Cataplana de tamboril at the Restaurante Solar do Peixe, showing the clips of the cooking vessel

The *cataplana* is a cooking utensil that is in the shape of two metal hemispheres that seal together using two clips. The *cataplana* is used on the top of the hob, and can be turned over to achieve even cooking. This method of cooking is traditionally from the Algarve, but is now used throughout Portugal.

If you prefer a simpler and more 'typical' restaurant, try **O Alcochetano** just next door (closed Mondays); this restaurant has plenty of grilled fresh fish and seafood.

In the centre of the town there is **O Cantinho do Ti-Tonho** (closed for dinner Monday and Tuesday), another restaurant with a 'típico' ambience and *fado* sessions on Sunday and Thursday evenings.

Our final recommendation is **Os Petiscos do António** (closed Tuesdays) in Largo Barão Samora Correia — a small pleasant restaurant offering Portuguese cuisine.

restaurants

eat

Óbidos was designated a National Monument in 1951. Just one look on arrival tells you why: it is an almost perfectly preserved medieval town, totally enclosed in the still-complete walls and topped off with a delightful little castle. You enter the town beneath this beautiful tiled gateway.

óbidos

EXCURSION

Óbidos is, deservedly, an extremely popular day trip destination from Lisbon, so it is easy to join one of the many guided tours on offer.

But it is less expensive and more fun to 'do your own thing' by going there on the very good bus service, and then wander around (and have lunch!) at your own pace, following your own interests.

Transport: 🚌 from Lisbon (Campo Grande, not on the plan, on the north side of the city, with metro station) to Óbidos. Departs Lisbon 08.15, 09.30, 12.00, 13.15; departs Óbidos 14.55, 16.10, 18.00; journey time 1h05min

Refreshments: at Óbidos (see page 135)

Area map: see page 134

Even better, if you are able to, spend a night there (the charming castle is nowadays a *pousada*) and then have time to explore this delightful town after the day trippers have gone, or before they arrive the next day.

You will find the **tourist office** just by the **bus terminal**. They have plenty of literature in English which will help you make up your own guided tour — you can even hire an audio guide for the day.

As you walk into the town from the bus terminal you will immediately be greeted with the town gate (**Porta da Vila**) shown opposite. This was the main access to the town from about 1380, when Óbidos was located on the coast (the silting up of the Rial Estuary in the 16th century created the Lagoa da Óbidos and has stranded the town some 11km inland). The gate shelters an oratory dedicated to the town's patron saint, Nossa Senhora da Piedade (17C) and has a remarkable tile covering dating from 1740-1745.

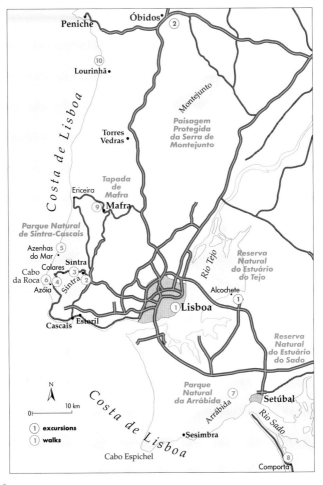

Peniche
Óbidos ②
⑩
Lourinhã •

Costa de Lisboa

Montejunto

*Paisagem
Protegida
da Serra de
Montejunto*

Torres
Vedras •

*Tapada
de
Mafra*

Ericeira
⑨ Mafra

*Parque Natural
de Sintra-Cascais*

Azenhas
do Mar • ⑤

Colares
Cabo ⑥ Sintra
da Roca ③
④ Sintra ②
Azóia

Cascais • Estoril

Rio Tejo

*Reserva
Natural
do Estuário
do Tejo*

• Alcochete ①

① Lisboa

*Reserva
Natural
do Estuário
do Sado*

N

0 ┤────── 10 km

① excursions
① walks

Costa de Lisboa

*Parque
Natural
da Arrábida* ⑦

Arrábida

Setúbal

Rio Sado

• Sesimbra

Cabo Espichel

Comporta ⑧

Óbidos: church of São Pedro and *nouvelle cuisine*, Portuguese-style, at Cozinha das Rainhas

Within the city walls of medieval Vila de Óbidos there are plenty of restaurants to choose from. But tucked away in the shelter of the wall itself is a restaurant offering typical regional Portuguese dishes in a '*nouvelle cuisine*' style: **Cozinha das Rainhas** in Rua Padre Nunes Tavares. Simple, but very pleasing ambiance, with unobtrusive classical background music. In summer you can eat outside on a patio beside the old walls. The restaurant (☎ 262 955 360; open daily) has a menu in English and takes credit cards.

Just *outside* the city walls, in Rua Porta do Vale, is the **Restaurante Ilustre Casa de Ramiro** (☎ 262 959 194; closed Thursdays). This restaurant has a wonderful medieval atmosphere. The décor is soft and subdued, with rich ochre pastel-coloured walls and ceiling. There is row of four huge storage pots along one wall, and the old kitchen fireplace gives added warmth to the place. The food doesn't disappoint either: we highly recommend the roast kid and turbot kebab.

restaurants

eat

BACALHAU

Bacalhau is such a fundamental ingredient in Portuguese cooking that no book claiming to feature Portuguese food could possibly avoid including at least one recipe for the famous codfish.

Every Portuguese housewife knows from childhood and parental tuition how to choose, prepare and cook the salted, dried cod. In fact each of these three steps is crucial to the success or failure of the final dish. One thing is certain: indifferently prepared, poor-quality *bacalhau* will give truly awful results! Good quality, well prepared *bacalhau* is a completely different story — immediately enjoyable, even to the non-Portuguese.

Selection
To the visitor, the piles of different qualities, prices, origins, etc can be totally bewildering. You will usually find some or all of the following qualities for sale:

   Corrente (average)
   Crescido (a bit better)
   Graúdo (substantially better)
   Especial ('special' — top quality)
   Asa Branca
   Cura Amarela

The first four are ranked in order of quality, starting with the basic. *Asa Branca* means that the dark inner lining of the 'wings' has been removed. The final designation means smoked. This obviously results in a very much stronger flavour — probably too strong for most foreign palettes.

recipes

eat

Traditionally, *bacalhau* came from the Grand Banks off New-foundland. Today most comes from Norway. The Portuguese will tell you that the best quality of all these days is from Iceland.

Whichever quality you select to use, the fish should be dry and hard.

Bacalhau — a bewildering selection

Preparation

This is almost as important as the initial selection. The key is to re-hydrate the flesh and remove the salt. This takes time. You will need to soak the fish for *at least* 24 hours, with several changes of water. Some recommend that the soaking be done under flowing water; others suggest that towards the end of the soaking process the fish should be put in milk for a final period of soaking, to further soften the flavour. After that, depending on the dish you are preparing, you will have to skin and bone the fish.

The quick way

These days you can avoid much of the above hassle (but miss the fun!) by buying ready-prepared *bacalhau* in the supermarket. This is called *bacalhau molhada*. It is sometimes found on the fish counter, or may be available frozen. It still has to be soaked, but for less time (as explained on the packets). At least all the skinning and de-boning has been done.

As we mention on page 9, one of Sunflower's requests was for us to search out wheat-, gluten- and dairy-free dishes. Food intolerances are becoming ever more common, and even for those who have learned to cope at home, it can be daunting to go on holiday. Rest assured that gf-df eating is very enjoyable around the Mediterranean and in Portugal, where olive oil, fish, tomatoes and 'alternative' grains and flours are basic to the diet. Many, many dishes are *naturally* gluten- and dairy-free.

EATING IN RESTAURANTS

The most common **first courses** are soup, fish and salads. Beware of *soups*; many are bread-based *(açordas)*. **Main courses** in this region feature fish and seafood, especially grilled, steaks, chops and roasts. Sauces *(molhos)* usually consist of wine, tomatoes, onions, herbs and garlic, all reduced rather than thickened with wheat flour (as you can see from our recipes). If you are a sauce addict, it is safer to *ask* (see inside back flap for help in Portuguese, although the staff usually speak English). *Fried* fish is invariably dusted with flour (otherwise it is more difficult to cook), but *ask:* they may be happy to do it for you without flour. All our recommended restaurants cook meals individually; the staff are always accessible. For **sweets**, try the gf, df Molotov pudding (page 43) or orange roll (page 91). All restaurants offer fruit (including many 'exotics'); some have gf, df chocolate dishes (made with dark chocolate); *ask!*

SELF-CATERING

While many hotels in Lisbon can cater for food intolerances — or will let you use their fridges (just label your container), consider self-catering (see page 14), so that you can try some of our recipes with the *authentic local* ingredients.

Gf, df shopping

Most of the large supermarkets have a 'Natural Food', section but the choice is very limited. So make for **Celeiro** in the Baixa area (25 on the plan), where you will find a very wide range of gf, df, vegetarian, vegan, macrobiotic and organic foods. Founded in 1974, Celeiro now has a chain of 13 shops (see their web site; they can, for instance, be found in most of the 'commercial centres'), but the one in Baixa is the best stocked.

The Baixa branch also has a **self-service restaurant**, open from 09.00-18.00 Mon-Fri, and, while the main emphasis is on vegetarian and vegan dishes, there is also a good selection for the gf, df diet. Menus are changed daily and even posted on their web site!

CELEIRO
Rua 1° de Dezembro, 65 (main branch); (210 306 030/fax 213 427 279
www.celeiro-dieta.pt
open Mon-Fri 09.00-18.00, Sat 09.00-13.00

Schar breads, pastas, biscuits, flours, cakes; also **Drei Pauly** and a few other gf purveyors not known in the UK — a great opportunity to sample new things!

Provamel soya drinks, sweets, cream, margarine

MENU DECODER

sopa soup

sopa de legumes vegetable soup
sopa de marisco seafood soup

peixe fish

amêijoas cockles
atum tuna
bacalhau dried codfish
camarão prawns
carapaus horse-mackerel
cherne turbot
dourada dory
enguia eel
gambas giant prawns
lagosta crayfish
langueirôes razor shell
lavagante lobster
linguado sole
lulas squid
marisco shellfish
mexilhões mussels
pargo sea-bream
peixe-espada swordfish
percebes barnacles
pescada whiting
polvo octopus
robalo sea-bass
rodovalho halibut

salmão salmon
salmonete red mullet
sapateira crab
sardinhas sardines
tamboril monkfish
truta trout

carne meat*

borrego lamb
carne de vaca beef
cabrito kid
coelho rabbit
faisão pheasant
fígado liver
frango chicken
leitão suckling-pig
pato duck
peru turkey
porco pork
vitela veal

*cuts of meat

costeletas cutlets, chops
lombo loin, sirloin
bife beefsteak, steak

*cooking methods

assado roast/baked
churrasco barbecued
cozido boiled
espetada kebab
estufado braised

frito fried
grelhado grilled
guisado stewed
na brasa grilled on hot coals
recheado stuffed

salada salad and legumes vegetables

abacate avocado
alface lettuce
alho garlic
batatas potatoes
cebola onion
cenoura carrot
cogumelos mushrooms
couve cabbage
ervilhas peas
espinafres spinach
feijão beans
pepino cucumber
pimento capsicum pepper
tomate tomato

fruta fruit

ananas/abacaxi pineapple
banana banana
laranja orange
limão lemon
maça apple
melão/meloa melon
morangos straw-berries
pêra pear
pêssego peach
uvas grapes

other menu items

açucar sugar
azeite olive oil
azeitonas olives
gelado ice-cream
leite milk
manteiga butter
paté paté
pão bread
pimenta pepper
piri-piri hot pepper sauce
presunto smoked ham
queijo cheese
sal salt
vinagre vinegar

SHOPPING ITEMS (for fish, meat, fruit and vegetables see menu decoder)

bacon *toucinho*
basil *manjerico*
bay (leaves) *louro (em folhas)*
beer *cerveja*
biscuits *bolachas*
bread *pão*
butter *manteiga*
cake *bolo*
cheese *queijo*
cider *sidra*
cinnamon *canela*
coffee *café*
coriander *coentros*

cream *natas*
curry powder *caril*
eggs *ovos*
flour (wheat) *farinha de trigo*
maize flour *farinha de milho*
corn flour *amido de milho*
fruit juice *sumo*
garlic *alho*
ham
  cooked *fiambre*
  smoked *presunto*
herbs *ervas*
honey *mel*
ice cream *gelado*
lard *banha*
milk *leite*

coconut milk *leite de côco*
mustard *mostarda*
nuts *nozes*
olive oil *aziete*
olives *azeitonas*
paprika (sweet) *colorau doce*
parsley *salsa*
pâté *pâté*
pepper *pimenta*
pepper (red) paste *massa de pimentão*
rice *arroz*
salt *sal*
sausage *salsicha*
  pork/ flour *alheira (farinheira)*

spicy *chouriço*
soup *sopa*
soya *soja*
spaghetti *esparguete*
spices, condiments *condimentos*
sugar *açucar*
tea *chá*
vinegar *vinagre*
wine *vinho*
  red *tinto*
  white *branco*
water *água*
  still *sem gás*
  sparkling *com gás*

CONVERSION TABLES

Weights		Volume		Oven temperatures		
						gas
10 g	1/2 oz	15 ml	1 tbsp	°C	°F	mark
25 g	1 oz	55 ml	2 fl oz			
50 g	2 oz	75 ml	3 fl oz	140°C	275°F	1
110 g	4 oz	150 ml	1/4 pt	150°C	300°F	2
200 g	7 oz	275 ml	1/2 pt	170°C	325°F	3
350 g	12 oz	570 ml	1 pt	180°C	350°F	4
450 g	1 lb	1 l	1-3/4 pt	190°C	375°F	5
700 g	1 lb 8 oz	1.5 l	2-1/2 pt	200°C	400°F	6
900 g	2 lb			220°C	425°F	7
1.35 g	3 lb			230°C	430°F	8
				240°C	475°F	9

Transport

The best way to get to Sintra from Lisbon is by **train** (about 30min). The normal departure point is Rossio station, but this is currently closed. In the meantime Sintra trains depart from Entrcampos or Sete Rios. The service is very frequent (every 10-15 minutes). For information concerning the re-opening of Rossio station (and train times if you need them) go to www.cp.pt. From Sintra station it is a good half-kilometre walk to the old centre, so you may prefer to jump on a Scott URB 433 or 434 bus.

Scott URB (www.scotturb.com) also runs an excellent **bus service** covering the Sintra/Cascais/Estoril area north of Lisbon. What's more, you can buy a combined train and bus travel card (€9.00 for one day), which will cover rail travel out from Lisbon to either Cascais or Sintra, where you can link up with the Scott URB bus network. For walks 4, 5 and 6 you will need to use 403 and 441 services of Scott URB. *Departures from Sintra and Cascais shown below are actual; arrival times approximate.*

Service 403

Departures from Sintra at 7.45*, 8.55, 10.25, 11.55, 13.25, 14.55, 15.45, 17.15, 18.25, 19.55; arrives Colares 20min later, Azóia 40min later, Cabo da Roca 45min later, Cascais 1h15min later

Departures from Cascais at 7.40*•, 9.07, 10.35, 12.05, 13.35, 14.25, 15.55, 17.05, 18.35, 19.45; arrives Cabo da Roca 31min later, Azóia 35min later, Colares 40min later, Sintra 1h05min later

Service 441

Departures from Sintra at 7.55, 9.10, 9.45, 10.40, 11.30•, 12.05, 13.00, 13.50, 14.30, 15.25, 16.30•, 16.50, 17.45, 18.28•, 18.45, 19.28, 20.30•, 21.00; arrives Colares 20min later; arrives Praia das Maças 26min later

Departures from Praia das Maças at 8.11•, 8.39, 9.59, 10.19, 11.19, 12.09•, 12.57, 13.49, 14.39, 15.14, 16.09, 17.04•, 17.39, 18.19, 19.12, 19.19•, 20.04, 21.04•

*does not stop at Cabo da Roca; •does not run on Sundays

bold type: photograph; *italic type:* map

INDEX

First edition © 2005
Published by Sunflower Books
PO Box 36061, London SW7 3WS
www.sunflowerbooks.co.uk

ISBN 1-85691-280-9

Cover photograph: Padrão dos Descobrimentos, Belém

Photographs: Paul Burton
Maps: John Underwood, adapted from Portuguese IGC and military maps
Series design: Jocelyn Lucas
Cookery editor: Marina Bayliss
A CIP catalogue record for this book is available from the British Library.
Printed and bound in Spain by Grafo Industrias Gráficas, Basauri

---

Before you go ...
log on to
www.sunflowerbooks.co.uk
and click on '**updates**', to see if we have been notified of any changes to
the routes or restaurants.

When you return ...
do let us know if any routes have changed because of road-building, storm
damage or the like. Have any of our restaurants closed — or any new ones
opened *on the route of the walk*? (Not Lisbon restaurants, please; these books
are not intended to be complete restaurant guides!)

Send your comments to mail@sunflowerbooks.co.uk
